Bureau of Curiosity

Question Everything

By Ed Morawski

Copyright 2019 by Ed Morawski

ISBN-10: 1712633228

ISBN-13: 978-1712633229

All rights reserved. No part or portion of this work may be reprinted, transmitted or used in any media without the written permission of the author.

Question Everything
Question Everything
Question Everything
Question Everything
Question Everything
Question Everything
Question Everything
Question Everything

Introduction

Answers to Questions You didn't Know You Had Because Everything You Thought You Knew Is Wrong

If Only I Knew Then What I Know Now...

It's an old saying, but so true. When we were children we knew nothing, we were a sponge ready to absorb whatever anyone (especially adults) told us. I never questioned my 'teachers'. How could I? They knew everything.

If you think about it, a large part of adulthood is unlearning most of what you were taught in childhood.

Your parents told you what they believed was true—whether it was really true or not.

Educators taught you what they were taught—even if they didn't really understand or had any clue something else existed.

And if you got some religious indoctrination, well all bets are off—you know what Church and Sunday school filled your head with.

You accepted all this as gospel because you were a kid and no one told you different. If you're a thinking person, how many times as an adult have you asked: 'Why didn't someone tell me this before?'

And if you're not, if you're the type that accepts what they've been told, that's a fatal flaw, a mistake that inhibits us all from thinking for ourselves.

There is a rule in computing: Garbage In, Garbage Out - the concept that flawed, or nonsense input data produces nonsense output.

So if, or more likely when, your parents and teachers fill your head with flawed garbage and beliefs, you will go around for the rest of your life under false pretences and making wrong decisions. And, just as bad, all that misinformation continues right to the present day.

It's kind of funny that very young children ask 'why' a lot but then it seems they lack the confidence to question things by the time they get to school.

The world would be a better place if everyone questioned everything.

With so much information available at our fingertips on the internet, you'd think we'd be living in a golden age of enlightenment, but it's the opposite – there is more nonsense floating around than ever. That's not to say the internet isn't a valuable source, there is good information if you know where to look. I wish I would have had it when I was a child. Today I wish someone would teach the kids how to use it and recognize the baloney from the steak.

Yes, of course I was in this mindset of just accepting everything I heard. It continued through Catholic school (oh boy, we'll go into

THAT later), the military (no room for independent thinkers there!), and into my thirties when I started raising a family (and continued to make the same mistakes with my children that plagued my own formative years).

It wasn't until I was deep in the corporate world, of all places, that cracks begin to develop in my wall of blind acceptance.

I met a gentleman by the name of Jerry O'Brien; my company brought him in as a telecommunications consultant and it just so happened he was given office space in my area of responsibility. Our company relied heavily on leased telephone lines for our business (alarm monitoring) – to the tunes of hundreds of thousands of dollars. Jerry claimed he could reduce that expense by auditing our phone bill.

He was right. (You have to put this in perspective because back then in the 1980s the world of telecommunications was a lot different than it is now. Telephone calls were expensive).

During his first week he showed me what he was doing. He went over our four hundred page phone bill line by line and found hundreds of errors: lines we were still paying for that had been canceled months or years before, lines that were mis-rated and charged incorrectly, erroneous toll charges, and on and on to the tunes of tens of thousands of dollars.

At first I couldn't accept this. I thought Mr. O'Brien was inflating the errors to increase his fee and reputation. The telephone company was an institution, like the government; the telephone company didn't make mistakes...

Oh, but they did. Soon the telephone company was begging for a meeting, they were in a total panic at all the errors O'Brien had found – and how much they were going to have to rebate our company.

Suddenly my belief in acceptance of the status quo was shattered. I began questioning everything in the corporate world.

Unfortunately, my focus was on the business side of life and it wasn't until my late fifties and early sixties that I turned my attention to the wider world around me. I opened my eyes and began questioning everything. I don't want you to wait so long. I want to open your eyes. At the very least I want you to learn to be skeptical.

We're going to question some of 'settled science' and widely held 'beliefs' using two of the most powerful tools available to humans:

Logic and common sense.

I don't want to bore you to death either so I'm limiting this exercise to a few areas of considerable current interest:

Where did we (humans) come from?

Is Climate Change real?

Why are Wildfires out of control?

What's Religion all about?

Which form of Government works?

Is Business good or bad?

Is there such a thing as Fate?

Don't get the idea I am anti-science as you read through this material. In fact, I am and always have been a major science buff. But I am much more acutely aware of what passes for science these days – not that the past was any better. If you look back you'll see how wrong science has been: 'The earth is the center of the universe' and 'The earth is flat' just to name two.

Science has been dead wrong about a lot of things and I'm pretty certain they still are wrong to this day. Any time you see or hear statements proclaiming something is 'settled science' or 'absolutely true', you can be fairly certain it isn't. The term 'impossible' I now know is just a viewpoint of the time period. A thousand years ago talking to or seeing someone on the other side of the world was impossible – plainly it isn't. 'Settled science', 'not possible', and 'absolute' are just excuse words for close minded people. And if anyone should know better – it is scientists.

It's amusing to me that people who call themselves scientists love to ridicule any theories outside of their own by slapping them with the term 'pseudo science'. They are quick to forget that the idea a light beam (a laser) could kill would have been pseudo science' just two hundred years ago – just like radio, television, and cell phones.

If I knew then what I know now - I would have asked a **LOT** of questions. One thing I do know is that we know very little about the universe and there are most certainly astounding discoveries to be made.

So prepare to be shocked as we question everything, and you discover everything you thought you knew is wrong.

1. Where Did We (Humans) Come From?

The drawing is meant as a joke (from bizarro.com) but it does represent scientific theory on the origin of humans.

The origin of humans is settled science; everyone knows we evolved from monkeys, right? I was taught that in school, a Catholic religious institution no less. I believed every word they told me. All the way back as far as Darwin, and through the Scopes Monkey Trial, science has maintained we humans evolved from monkeys.

[Note that evolutionists lost the Scopes trial by the way]

Well, not so fast there buckaroo, it turns out if you scratch the surface just a little with your thumbnail, there are many, many questions and very, very few answers.

If humans evolved from monkeys, why are monkeys still around?

This is the question that began to pry open my mind.

And it should be a simple question. Evolution is defined as the process by which different kinds of living organisms are thought to have developed and diversified from earlier forms during the history of the earth.

This picture is supposed to show how humans evolved. About the only similarity I see is that all have two legs.

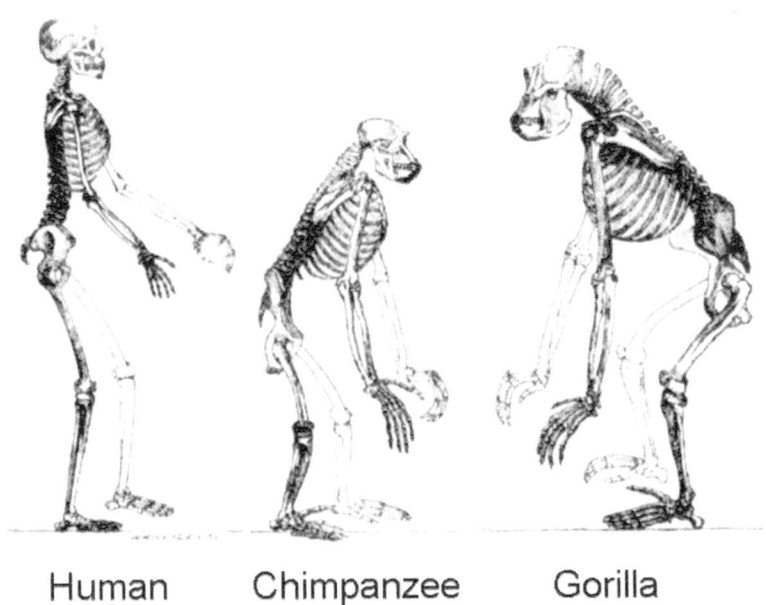

Human   Chimpanzee   Gorilla

Evolution is the process of evolving – changing from one form to another. So if humans evolved from monkeys, how can monkeys still be here with us? Why didn't all monkeys become humans?

Oh this question will get you ridiculed fast. But if you type this exact question into Google you will notice a lot of people asked the same thing and you will get a lot of results. You will also quickly notice that the 'answer' is steeped in the refuge of semantics:

"Humans did not evolve from monkeys. Instead, monkeys and humans share a common ancestor from which both evolved around 25 million years ago," says Dr Paul Willis, paleontologist and Director of RIAus. At which he launches into an explanation of our erroneous question:

"This question reveals a couple of fundamental misunderstandings about evolution and how it operates."

[He's saying we're too ignorant to ask this question!!!]

"Firstly, humans did not evolve from monkeys. Instead, monkeys and humans share a common ancestor from which both evolved around 25 million years ago."

"This evolutionary relationship is supported both by the fossil record and DNA analysis. A 2007 study showed that humans and rhesus monkeys share about 93% of their DNA. Based on the similarities and differences between the two types of DNA, scientists have estimated that humans and rhesus monkeys diverged from their common ancestor 25 million years ago.

[25 **million** years? Show me a human fossil from 25 million years ago!]

"Similarly, the fossil record has identified ancestors common to both humans and monkeys, such as an as yet unnamed primate fossil from Myanmar found in 2009 and dated as living around 37 million years ago.

"Humans are actually more closely related to chimpanzees and other apes, but DNA evidence again shows that <u>we didn't evolve from them.</u> Chimps and humans share between 98 to 99% of DNA suggesting that we shared a common ancestor around 6 million years ago."

[Oh really? So now we didn't evolve from chimps either? And now it's 6 million years? I thought humans were only around about 300,000 years? The earliest fossils of anatomically similar humans are from the Middle Paleolithic, about 300-200,000 years ago such as the Omo remains of Ethiopia – [Human – Wikipedia]

[Confused yet? And – the fact these guys never seem to get around to letting us know is that they never found any direct or indirect fossil link between apes and humans. The so-called 'missing link' has never been found. Yet we have fossils before and after the period when this 'link' supposedly lived.]

"The idea of sharing a common ancestor leads to the second major misunderstanding inherent in the question," says Dr Willis, "that evolution is a linear process where one species evolves into another."

"Evolution is really a branching process where one species can give rise to two or more species.

"The fallacy of linear evolution is most clearly illustrated by the analogy of asking; how can I share common grandparents with my cousins if my cousins and my grandparents are still alive?" says Dr Willis. "The answer is of course that your grandparents had more than one child and they each went off and started their own families creating new branches of your own family tree."

[This has to be one of the most stupid and condescending statements I have ever heard. He is equating offspring to evolution. And nobody questions it? This is exactly my point – we tend to blindly accept what some 'educated' person is telling us!]

So ask the question differently: if humans evolved from apes, how come apes are still around? You'll get the same nonsense results: humans and apes split somewhere along the line. That's like saying present day tigers and saber tooth tigers split somewhere along the line – except there are no saber tooth tigers around, are there? In fact, name any animal alive today that evolved from something else and that 'something else' is not still alive today.

There are so many problems with this theory it's mind boggling.

And if all this is confusing, well maybe that's because science is all over the map on human evolution. Let's say for the sake of argument that Chimpanzees and humans did split into separate species 25 million or 6 million or whatever years ago. Why would that happen? Why would 'Nature' split apes and humans, for what possible purpose? Ape-like creatures were doing just fine, why didn't they evolve completely into humans?

But again, let's say the two did split. Well then, did two human-like creatures suddenly appear simultaneously? Either they did – which is against all odds, or early humans mated with apes – how else did the human line continue? It would obviously require a male and female living at exactly the same moment to propagate the human race. Or there were ape-human hybrids running around for thousands of years until another being evolved into a companion male or female. Messy isn't it?

Look at it from another angle: If apes and humans split 25 million years ago, and if apes are so much like us they can be taught sign language, then why didn't they evolve into human-like beings? Could it be that apes will evolve into intelligent beings in another million years? If so then why did humans 'evolve' so much faster?

There are clearly more questions than answers.

The fact is that no matter what they tell you, modern physically similar beings (anatomically modern humans), really didn't exist until 11,500 years ago (11.5 ka, beginning of the Holocene period). Although older fossils are called Homo sapiens, they don't look anything like us today except they have two legs.

Lately scientists have claimed fossils attributed to Homo sapiens, along with stone tools, dated to approximately 300,000 years ago. Found at Jebel Irhoud, Morocco they represent the earliest fossil evidence for 'anatomically modern' Homo sapiens. But that is clearly not true - even though our esteemed scientists call Jebel Irhoud a Homo sapien, you can look at the photo and clearly see a very pronounced brow extension.

It still doesn't look like us!

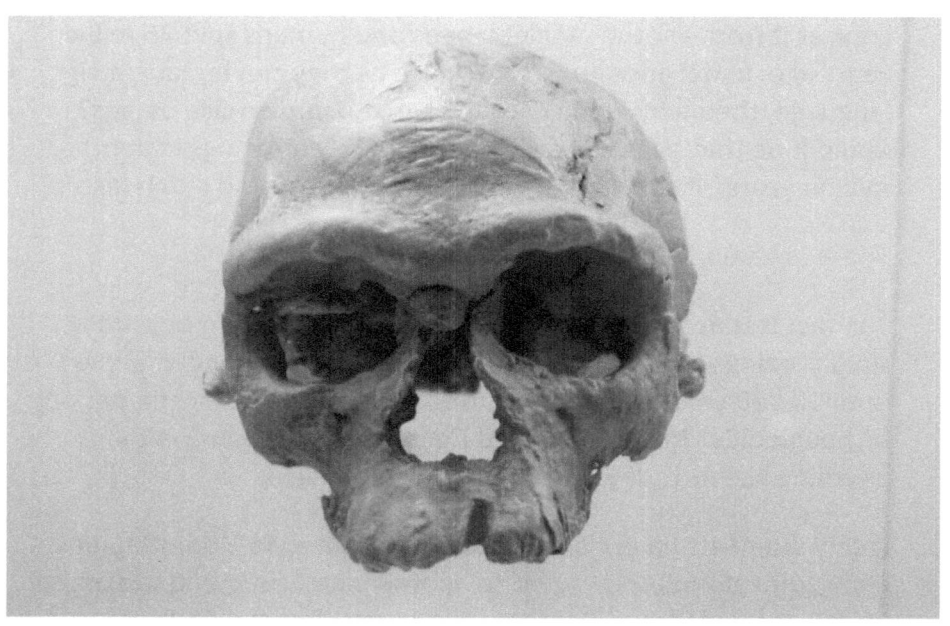

If you want to have some fun just ask Google for the 'oldest human fossil'. You'll get wildly differing ages ranging from 25 million years to 11,500 years. Note that the vast majority are not 'human' as we would recognize them. They are merely hominid upright walkers – just like apes.

Recent studies have claimed our DNA is shared with some of these 300,000 year old beings, but if you look closely it becomes obvious these results are strained at best. Exceedingly minute DNA samples scraped off 300,000 year old fossils are 'calculated' and 'extrapolated' and 're-sequenced' – all fudge words seemingly geared towards proving their point. And these types of DNA tests are not like the method used in criminal trials, no these are basically working backwards, like proving a negative.

Science also claims we share 96% - 99% of our DNA with apes, but 98% of our DNA is junk or 'noncoding' (pc term). Think about that for a minute. At best 2% of 99% of our DNA is shared with apes. So what's all the rest of it? Answer: completely UNKNOWN!

Here's a quote from Medical Life Science News:

'DNA contains instructions (coding) that are used to create proteins in the cell. However, the amount of DNA contained inside each cell is vast and not all of the genetic sequences present within a DNA molecule actually code for a protein.

'Some of this noncoding DNA is used to produce non-coding RNA components such as transfer RNA, regulatory RNA and ribosomal RNA. However, other DNA regions are not transcribed into proteins, nor are they used to produce RNA molecules and their function is unknown.'

'The proportion of coding versus noncoding DNA varies significantly between species. In the human genome for example, almost all (98%) of the DNA is noncoding, while in bacteria, only 2% of the genetic material does not code for anything.'

So science tells us – with a straight face – DNA proves we evolved from apes. They're absolutely certain apes and humans are 96% the same, but have no clue about the other 98% of our DNA.

Science can claim humans were around for 25 million years because 2% of DNA is similar but really they were ape-like creatures bearing no resemblance to humans except they walked on two legs.

In reality the true age of humans as we know them today is more like 11,500 years - maybe. If you count wearing clothes, having a language, and using fire as <u>real traits of human beings</u>, then those beings haven't been here long at all. The actual first civilization where humans had language and written cuneiform communication was only 3,000 BC (5,000 years ago) in Sumer, located in Mesopotamia. This is the first known complex civilization, developing the first city-states in the 4th millennium BCE. The Sumerian language from 3,000 BC is one of the earliest known written languages.

If all this is confusing and doesn't make much sense, it's because it doesn't – that's my point.

So what is the Point of how old humans are?

Because if us humans are only 11,500 years old it would explain a heck of a lot of anomalies.

There are only two possibilities of how humans came to exist on earth.

1 – We crawled out of the ocean as some salamander-like creature 500 million years ago, became apes (oh excuse me – ape-like creatures) and evolved into us.

2 – Someone or something put us here.

If you believe in God or a Supreme Being creator then just maybe the Garden of Eden wasn't a place, but a state of mind. Maybe 11,000 years ago a male and a female were created (by some Supreme Being Creator God) and lived in the paradise of an unspoiled earth with endless resources. Maybe they lost their way and it wasn't until 3,000 BC they were able to regain some semblance of normal life.

Or – much more likely – someone brought us here 11,000 years ago to colonize earth.

A lot of people (and maybe you) laugh at this notion.

The truth is that there are signs of this everywhere that mainstream science chooses to ignore.

Every ancient civilization on earth left behind drawings, carvings, pictograms, statutes, and artifacts depicting strange beings in flying machines. Egyptian art is full of them - like hieroglyphs in the 3,000-year-old Temple of Seti in Abydos, Egypt (seen below). Almost all indigenous peoples all over the globe have left behind similar artifacts. You can see photos of these objects all over the internet and decide for yourself.

I promised we would use logic and common sense to examine some of these questions, so here goes.

If humans are 25 million years old, why have we never adapted to our own sun?

The sun will blind us, it will burn us, it causes cancer, and it will kill us. How can that be? Wouldn't we have evolved protection – like all the other living organisms on earth? Even those early Homo sapiens had pronounced brow ridges to shield their eyes from the sun's glare – why don't we today?

Birds don't mind the sun; mammals seem to get along just fine. Cats bask in a sunny window. Virtually all wildlife lives outside exposed to the sun all day. Most of these animals have fur and special eyelids that protect them, but not humans. Why?

Why would evolution discard fur on humans when it is so vital in protecting us from sun and cold? Mother Nature doesn't make mistakes like that. What possible reason would humans evolve to shed fur? The earth has gone through several ice ages, you'd think for that reason alone we'd still have fur, let alone as protection from the constant sun.

How can our own sun be so dangerous to us – especially after 25 million years? It makes no sense whatsoever – unless we haven't been on earth for 25 million or even 300,000 years. It only makes sense if we didn't originate here, if we are very late arrivals and haven't had time to adapt (or evolve) protection from harmful UV rays.

Let's look at this another way.

Everyone is familiar with the dragonfly; they live almost everywhere on earth. Did you know dragonflies are at least 320 million years old? Yes, an intact fossil of an imprint of a dragonfly has been found in rock known to be 320 million years old. And it is virtually identical to the dragonfly of today! In other words the dragonfly has undergone NO evolution in at least 320 million years. It was created so perfectly that no modification through evolution or mutation was needed.

And dragonflies are hardly the only beings that never 'evolved' –

alligators, crocodiles, and cockroaches, to name a few, share that trait.

If evolution is real where did the octopus come from?

See, you didn't even know that was in question did you? Well it turns out cephalopods (octopuses, squids, and cuttlefish) developed so weirdly they may have evolved in a different ecosystem – outside of earth. The Octopus family is like nothing else on earth.

"The octopus genome is comparable to the human genome in complexity, except it has a far greater number of protein-coding genes — some 33,000, compared with fewer than 25,000 in humans", says Alison Abbott in an issue of Nature.

In 2017 scientists discovered that octopuses, along with some squid and cuttlefish species, routinely edit their own RNA (ribonucleic acid) sequences to adapt to their environment.

This is weird because that's really not how adaptations usually happen in multi-cellular animals. When an organism changes in some fundamental way, it typically starts with a genetic mutation - a change to the DNA.

Those genetic changes are then translated into action by DNA's molecular sidekick, RNA. You can think of DNA instructions as a recipe, while RNA is the chef that orchestrates the cooking in the kitchen of each cell, producing necessary proteins that keep the whole organism going. So cephalopods didn't 'evolve' by mutation like everything else, they seemed to have adapted themselves.

https://evolutionnews.org/2015/08/octopus_genome/

The bottom line is scientists have no consensus on how squids and octopuses evolved or where they came from. This is another nail in the coffin of 'settled science' when it comes to how life originated on earth.

These following two articles are interesting – and amusing. The first speculates cephalopods are so different and unique from any other organism, they must have originated somewhere besides earth. The second ridicules that notion – without ever explaining where they did come from. In other words the idea is too silly to take seriously, even though the evidence suggests otherwise. Just another example of 'scientists' sticking their heads in the sand.

https://qz.com/1281064/a-controversial-study-has-a-new-spin-on-the-otherworldliness-of-the-octopus/

https://www.livescience.com/62594-octopuses-are-not-aliens-panspermia.html

Even more troubling is the problem that no TRUE transitional fossils have ever been found for ANY species on earth. Wikipedia only lists SIX and they are all questionable. If any of you reading this are still in school or university, ask your teacher or instructor or professor about transitional fossils and see what blank stares you get or more likely a brush off. Science can't even definitively say what birds evolved from.

Yet we are expected to believe that after 25 million years humans still are not adapted to our environment, let alone perfect in any sense of the word.

Personally, I feel 'natural selection' is absolutely real, but the jury is still out on evolution.

Let's just assume humans have been here for 25 million years. Just for the sake of argument, let's pretend there was only one human born and deceased every 30 years (the normal lifespan in the savage wilderness of early earth).

25 million years / 30 years = 833,333 iterations of one human. Now let's say there was a steady total world human population of 100,000 during these 25 million years.

833,333 X 100,000 = 83,333,333,333.

That's 83 billion chances to get humans perfect. So nature failed 83 billion times?

Now think about just the last hundred years of human existence.

We invented steam engines, railroads, internal combustion engines, autos, airplanes, electricity, batteries, jet engines, rockets, vacuum tubes, transistors, digital circuits, lasers, radio, radar, GPS, telephones, cell phones, television, atomic energy, computers, tablets, traveled into space, and on and on.

Humans did all that in 0.000004% the time it supposedly took us to evolve? I find it incredibly hard to believe that we accomplished more in 100 years than in 25,000,000 years. It doesn't make logical sense. Isn't evolution linear? How could we evolve so little in 25 million years and so quickly in just one hundred years?

There are more questions.

If Humans evolved from fish how come we can't swim naturally?

or

Since our planet earth is 71% water, why didn't we

evolve better suited to live in water?

Just like the sun water will kill us. We can't live in it for more than a few minutes without artificial means – yet three quarters of our home is water. There are plenty of mammals like alligators that are perfectly suited to living in the water and on land. Humans are the dominant species on earth, why didn't we evolve the ability to live anywhere and everywhere? Or at the very least know how to swim when we are born?

It would seem humans are entirely unsuited to live and thrive on earth – unlike every other living organism here. We can't or won't eat most of the plants that grow naturally wild. When is the last time you had a nice helping of Amaranth, Burdock, or Field Pennycress? Almost all of vegetables we do eat (when we are forced to) have been artificially modified. We are not really designed to eat meat – our teeth and jaws are suited for vegetation and clearly meat is bad for us. It's as though humans don't belong here.

Why are we humans so violent?

I don't think I need to convince anyone of this. Violence is all around us. Humans have a history of violence since at least 3,000 BC. The Bible documents it. Violence continued through the time of Christ, the middle ages, world wars – just think of all the battles that have been fought through history. Why? What is it about us that causes us to destroy, cheat, lie, steal, beat, rape, and murder? Humans are by and large the most savage beasts on this planet. It would seem we are genetically wired to commit violence. There is no logical answer. Humans are violent, and that is a fact, sad as it may be.

Hold that thought.

A documentary on PBS/Nova called 'The Violence Paradox' recently made the outlandish claim violence has declined to almost nothing today. This notion seems to have originated from liberal Progressives, mostly in the guise of Professor Steven Pinker, who maintain we are no longer violent and now live in the most peaceful time in human history. I sat through an hour of this with my mouth open trying to come to terms with what I was hearing and seeing. My suspicions grew as I noticed how labored the terminology seemed. The presenters never talked numbers – only percentages.

For example, violent deaths of all kinds have declined from around 500 per 100,000 people per year before the time of Christ to around 50 per 100,000 in the middle Ages. Today, the numbers are down to 6-8 per 100,000 worldwide. The documentary also was heavily focused on as far back as 10,000 years – when absolutely no records were kept.

[One scientist even casually pointed out what he claimed was a 200,000 year old human skull with evidence of a violent death. As I've said previously there were no humans like us running around 200,000 years ago – they were apes for all intents and purposes.]

Eventually the show finally displayed some charts and I realized how they were making these ridiculous claims about a 99.9% reduction in violent deaths. They weren't counting **INDIVIDUAL** deaths they were counting deaths per 100,000 of population.

Oh, sure, back in 550 BC 100,000 people were killed in the Persian Wars but there were estimated to be only 100 million alive on the earth.

What a bunch of baloney! Leave to the scientists to twist facts just like they've learned to do on climate change.

If you look at the **NUMBER** of violent deaths, the twentieth century was far and away the most violent in all of history – and these numbers are only due to war, other violent deaths aren't counted:

WW1	110 million
Russian Civil War	9 million
Chinese Civil War	11 million
Sino – Japanese War	25 million
WW2	85 million
Korean War	4 million
Vietnam War	3 million
Nigerian Civil War	3 million
Bangladesh War	3 million
War in Afghanistan	2 million
2nd Sudanese War	2 million
2nd Congo War	5 million

2016 No wars just 500,000 violent deaths.

Even though the percentage has gone down, the numbers have gone way up. About the only fact they got right was that males (sorry gender word haters) were responsible for 97% of all violent acts. One scientist even suggested with a smirk – if we could just get rid of men we'd be fine.

So let's get back to reality – humans are extremely violent people.

Now here is the second part of my point:

Astronomers tell us there are billions of planets in just our galaxy, let alone the universe, that could support life. Why haven't we met any other intelligent beings?

The Search for Extra-Terrestrial Intelligence (SETI) has been going on since 1980, since there should be billions of civilizations out there, why haven't any responded? If science is correct, then the odds are overwhelmingly in favor of contact with aliens, but there has been nothing.

Maybe they hear us just fine - but don't want to contact us?

Now put two and two together.

Humans don't seem to be suited to live on earth. No other aliens have ever contacted us. There could be a very logical answer:

Earth is a prison.

Just suppose sometime in the past 11,500 years ago the 'Star Federation' or whatever group of beings on those vast numbers of other worlds call themselves, deemed humans too violent to coexist with other races. So they dumped the last remaining of us on a distant planet in the far off corner of the universe called earth. Sound familiar - like Australia for example?

Maybe we were exiled here, left with a few meager supplies and tools to fend for ourselves, fighting off predators, the sun, the ocean; and learning to eat what was available. And all the descendants of those first prisoners forever after worshipped the gods that came from the sky, praying they would return and take us back home- to our Garden of Eden.

Suddenly it all fits, all the anomalies are explained.

Maybe UFO sightings are sentries checking to make sure we're still in our prison. Maybe the reason UFOs never communicate with anyone is because they're merely prison guards who hate us. Maybe the reason we've never been back to our moon is because we were warned away from ever trying to escape. Maybe the reason governments cover up UFO sightings is because they know the truth.

Governments are not afraid revealing UFOs are real because we can't handle the idea of other life in the universe – no, they're quite rightly afraid of what would happen if we all found out we were prisoners on our planet.

Now a lot makes sense – common sense and logical.

Humans don't seem well adapted to earth.

Humans have not been here that long.

Humans are extremely violent.

The odds are great there is other intelligent life in the universe, but we have never had contact.

UFO sightings have been happening for thousands of years.

Humans could never accept we are prisoners.

2. Climate Change

Is it global warming or global cooling this decade?

Oh, let's call it climate 'change' – that way the climate activists will be right no matter which way it goes. Did you notice that subtle change in terminology a few years ago – from 'global warming' to 'climate change'? That's because they looked rather silly holding conferences on global warming when outside it was snow covered and freezing. Funny how no one mentions we've had some severely cold winters the past few years.

This topic is bound to get me a few haters. Oh, climate change is real alright, but it certainly isn't caused by humans no matter how many 'studies' and altered data certain so-called scientists produce. The fact is the earth has been going through climate cycles since it was first formed and it will continue to do so until our sun burns out.

See https://en.wikipedia.org/wiki/Geologic_temperature_record **and** https://en.wikipedia.org/wiki/List_of_periods_and_events_in_climate_history

The current state of climate change paranoia is the biggest hoax ever perpetrated on human kind since science claimed the earth was flat. And we all fall for it despite overwhelming evidence and factual data that the earth has always gone through climate cycles.

The laughable part is that science itself has documented proof of these past climate change cycles but chooses to ignore them and claim humans are causing it.

We humans never, ever learn from our past. We pay no attention to history and thus are destined to repeat the same mistakes over and over. The current generation has completely forgotten or overlooked the glaring, blaring headlines and warnings of the 1970's proclaiming global cooling – that we were on the verge of a new Ice Age. In the June 24, 1974 issue, Time presented an article titled "Another Ice Age?"

Descendents of those same scientists now scream - just 50 years later - we are in a period of global warming and life as we know it will be over in twelve years (or less).

All this despite them knowing full well climate cycles last hundreds of thousands of years – not a few decades. The exact age of the human race may be in doubt but science has probably nailed the age of earth at 4.5 billion years. That's billions with a 'B'. For anyone to claim we are in one period or another from the viewpoint of a few decades is so silly as to be laughable, not to mention unbelievably egomaniacal. Come back and tell me in 100,000 years what cycle we were in because anything less than thousands of years is a wild ass guess and all the scientists know it. When it comes to earth's geological and climate cycles they are measured in millennia and not tiny decades.

But they all blame this 'change' on human activity. We can't very well have caused global cooling so I guess warming is the next best thing!

Now think about this subject logically. Notice no climate scientist or activist ever uses the word WEATHER in conjunction with climate change. Why? Because how could humans really affect the weather? Well we haven't been able to control the weather yet (despite trying for a hundred years – remember seeding clouds?), yet that is exactly what scientists are claiming – that we are causing GLOBAL weather warming. In order to cause global warming you'd have to have the ability to control or at least change the WEATHER. It's preposterous and ludicrous that humans could possibly cause global temperature change.

The sad part is that scientists have so bought into this in order to fund their own careers that they will stop at nothing – including 'correcting' worldwide temperature readings (always upwards) to make their case.

In fact no one knows why the earth goes through climate cycles of cold and hot. Evidence suggests that the period of 2,000 to 3,000 million years ago was very generally colder and more glaciated than the last 500 million years. This is thought to be the result of solar radiation approximately 20% lower than today. Solar luminosity was 30% dimmer when the Earth formed 4.5 billion years ago, and it is expected to increase in luminosity approximately 10% per billion years in the future. In other words the sun is getting brighter and that's why the temperature (may be) rising at the rate of ½ degree a year.

Don't believe that bull dinky that you see on news casts every month that "last month was the hottest on record". Actually, the hottest dates and months on record were back in 1909 – long before any kind of greenhouse gases were invented.

The highest registered air temperature on Earth was 56.7 °C (134.1

°F) in Furnace Creek Ranch, California, located in the Death Valley desert in the United States, on July 10, 1913. Some scientists don't believe that one and use this:

July 11, 1909   57.8 °C (136.0 °F) Cherokee, Oklahoma

Doesn't really matter, both dates are prior to manmade greenhouse gases.

Also note that every current temperature timeline begins in 1880.

Years	Temperature	Change from previous
1880–1889	−0.493 °F	N/A
1890–1899	−0.457 °F	-0.0360 °F
1900–1909	−0.466 °F`	−0.00900 °F
1910–1919	−0.497 °F	−0.0306 °F
1920–1929	−0.315 °F	+0.182 °F
1930–1939	−0.0774 °F	+0.238 °F
1940–1949	0.0630 °F	+0.140 °F
1950–1959	−0.0360 °F	−0.0990 °F
1960–1969	−0.0252 °F	+0.0108 °F
1970–1979	−0.00180 °F	+0.0234 °F
1980–1989	0.317 °F	+0.319 °F
1990–1999	0.563 °F	+0.247 °F)
2000–2009	0.923 °F	+0.360 °F
2010–2019	1.32 °F	+0.477 °F

Notice the earth was supposedly cooling between 1880 – 1980 even though the hottest temperatures on record – on the entire earth – were in 1909 and 1913. We're also supposed to believe that back in 1900, for example, they could drop a thermometer from a ship into the ocean and actually measure a −0.00900 °F difference.

Also note that the temperature increase over the past 40 years was a whopping .477 degrees – not even half a degree. So basically if the boatswain's mate back in 1889 misread his thermometer by 0.0360 °F because his eyes were blurry from too much grog the night before, 1889 could have been the warmest year on record and 2019 the coldest. That's the kind of data we're talking about here. That's the SETTLED SCIENCE people scream about.

And by the way, we're just as likely to get another Ice Age as a global warming period – since no one has any idea what caused the three previous Ice Ages earth has undergone. We've (maybe) had forty years of warming but 100 years of cooling in the past 140 years. That doesn't seem like scientific proof the world is coming to end.

The last 3 million years have been characterized by cycles of glacials and interglacials within a gradually deepening ice age. Currently, the Earth is in an interglacial period, beginning about 20,000 years ago.

The cycles of glaciation involve the growth and retreat of continental ice sheets in the Northern Hemisphere and involve fluctuations on a number of time scales, notably on the 21,000, 41,000, and 100,000 year scales. Such cycles are usually interpreted as being driven by predictable changes in the Earth orbit known as Milankovitch cycles. At the beginning of the Middle Pleistocene (0.8 million years ago, close to the Brunhes–Matuyama geomagnetic reversal) there has been a largely unexplained switch in the dominant periodicity of glaciations from the 41,000 to the 100,000 year cycle.

The gradual intensification of this ice age over the last 3 million years has been associated with declining concentrations of the greenhouse gas carbon dioxide, though it remains unclear if this change is sufficiently large to have caused the changes in temperatures. Decreased temperatures can cause a decrease in carbon dioxide as, by Henry's Law, carbon dioxide is more soluble in colder waters, which may account for 30ppmv of the 100ppmv decrease in carbon dioxide concentration during the last glacial maximum.

The media has wholeheartedly bought into this climate change business and is extremely fond of showing endless videos and photos of icebergs breaking off at the poles as absolute proof of global warming. Ah, do they recall the Titanic? It sank in 1916 – from running into a **massive iceberg**.

And all those photos of icebergs – perhaps someone should remind the media the camera wasn't invented until 1816 and the first photographs of glaciers weren't until the 1880s – so obviously there is absolutely no proof the poles haven't been expanding or melting before the 1800s.

We've only been able to visually document events for the past 150 years – that's not even a blip on the earth climate cycle. Earth's climate cycles are measured in millions of years not a few decades.

In summary 'Concerned Scientists' are absolutely convinced without question that human activity is causing global warming (excuse me, 'climate change'), because they have irrefutable proof the earth has warmed by .477 degrees F over the past 40 years – despite the fact the earth has undergone climate change cycles for millions of years.

That sounds real scientific: base an assumption on 40 years out of 4.5 billion...

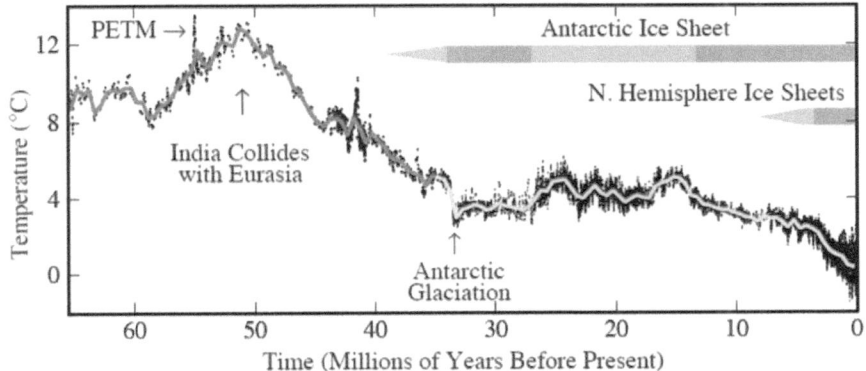

So it is quite possible the earth is cooling not warming. If you look at the past in millions of years you will notice the earth has been cooling since it was formed. Too bad none of the strident climate scientists yelling the world is over won't be alive to get the egg on their faces when we all freeze because of a natural climate cycle.

See how stupid all this climate change nonsense really is? Here's a recent example of 'news' headlines from the same outlet – USA Today one day apart. Apparently they don't read their own news or more likely can't get their story straight. We went from climate warming to climate cooling in 24 hours:

USA TODAY November 7, 2019, 11:09 AM PST

One of the world's thickest mountain glaciers is melting because of global warming, a new analysis reports.

USA TODAY November 8, 2019, 5:34 AM PST

Next week's Arctic blast will be so cold, forecasters expect it to break 170 records across US, This week's cold snap is only an appetizer compared with the main Arctic blast that's coming next week, meteorologists said. That freeze could be one for the record books.

Huh?

At some point in the climate change saga we need to discuss pollution since that is supposedly how humans are affecting the weather.

I'll go on record right here that it is not a good idea to pollute our air, water, or land. It is very dumb to spew toxic chemicals into our air. It is even dumber to dump them into our water or bury them in our land. And we absolutely must recycle everything possible.

How stupid can humans really be?

We are the only beings on earth (and probably in the universe) to poison our own home.

We shouldn't even need laws about this; everyone should want to keep our environment clean.

So why don't we? Greed, plain and simple. It's cheaper to spew that smoke into the air then clean it. It's cheaper to dump toxic waste into a river then clean it. No doubt this is part of our violence prone nature since greed goes hand in hand with stealing.

With that being said are these actions responsible for climate change? I seriously doubt it. Besides, as long as there are major polluters like China. No one state is going to have much impact on the situation.

Here is a case in point – from the most famous smoggiest city in the world:

New satellite measurements show how polluted Los Angeles' air

really is by Amina Khan

https://phys.org/news/2019-11-satellite-polluted-los-angeles-air.html

'Scientists who scanned the skies above dozens of U.S. cities have made a surprising discovery about the smog that's suspended over Los Angeles: one of its key ingredients isn't disappearing as fast as it once did.

"That's certainly part of why we're in a moment in Los Angeles where it's harder to get the air cleaner," said Ronald Cohen, an atmospheric chemist at UC Berkeley who reported the findings in the journal Science.

Nitrogen oxides—a combination of nitric oxide (NO) and nitrogen dioxide (NO_2) - are generated by motor vehicles and industrial machines like power plants, boilers, turbines and cement kilns.

When NOx molecules are mixed with volatile organic compounds—from vehicles and a vast array of household and commercial products—and exposed to sunlight, they help form pollutants like ozone.

NOx emissions have fallen at a rate of roughly 7% a year from 2006 to 2013 across most U.S. cities, Cohen said. Scientists had presumed there was a direct correlation between those emissions and NOx levels in the air.

The study used satellite data to measure nitrogen dioxide—a good proxy for nitrogen oxides as a whole—in 28 U.S. cities, including Memphis, Indianapolis and New York. They focused on city centers, presumably the epicenter of the area's NOx emissions, and measured how quickly those levels dropped with distance.

It turned out that the length of time the molecules stuck around in the atmosphere before being broken down by chemical reactions seemed to follow different patterns over time in different cities.

In cities like Los Angeles, Memphis and Washington D.C., those NOx lifetimes fell from 2006 until around 2010. Then they started to creep up again. [Despite all the regulations.]

This could help explain why, after years of steady drops in the overall amount of NOx in Los Angeles' air, that decline began to slow around 2010 and almost level out through 2013, the most recent year covered in the study.

The emissions cuts in Los Angeles do seem to have made a big difference. Taking the NOx lifetime changes into account, the researchers estimated that there were more than 41 metric tons of NOx in the air above L.A. in 2006; by 2010, there were around 27 metric tons. That was the largest drop among all the cities over that time period. However, since 2010, the decline slowed and nearly flattened, dropping only to 25 metric tons in 2013.

That left Los Angeles with NOx levels high above second-place Chicago (with nearly 17 metric tons) and third-place Detroit (just under 12 metric tons).

When the scientists looked at the concentrations of NOx in each city's air, New York reigned supreme in 2013, at 4.7 quadrillion molecules per square centimeter. Chicago was next, with 4.1 quadrillion; Los Angeles came in third, with 4 quadrillion.'

[The fact is that Los Angeles has the strictest pollution regulations in the world. The Air Quality Board regulates paint booths and even barbeque grill emissions. Burning of any kind is prohibited. Yet despite the LA area having the toughest laws and Chicago and Detroit having NONE, LA is still the smoggiest city in the U.S. What does that tell you?]

Still not convinced? Well consider this:

All of the earth's deserts were once fertile land. That's right, there probably were no deserts on earth – until 8,000 – 10,000 years ago. Climate activists and 'concerned scientists' would have you believe that the current warming trend is a recent human caused event.

There is much evidence to the contrary:

Mojave Desert

New research suggests that a desert region in the western U.S. – including Nevada, Utah, Oregon, and parts of California — was a rather damp setting until approximately 8,200 years ago, when the region began to dry out, eventually assuming the arid environments we see today. The study was published in the journal Quaternary Science Reviews in June, 2015.

All around the deserts of Utah, Nevada, southern Oregon, and eastern California, ancient shorelines line the hillsides above dry valley floors, like bathtub rings, remnants of the lakes once found throughout the region. Even as the ice sheets retreated at the end of the last ice age, 12,000 years ago, the region remained much wetter than it is today. The earliest settlers of the region are likely to have encountered a verdant landscape of springs and wetlands.

Arabian Desert

When most of us think of Arabia, we think of rolling sand dunes, scorching sun, and precious little water. But in the quite recent past it was a place of rolling grasslands and shady woods, watered by torrential monsoon rains. The first wet phase happened between 160,000 and 150,000 years ago, and the most recent was around

55,000 years ago.

Australia Outback

Research shows that before about 50,000 years ago, much of Australia's interior was a very different place to the scatter of salt-crusted lakes and sand ridges seen today. Back then perennial inland rivers fed huge, permanent mega-lakes.

The scene probably featured more vegetation than today, large herbivores and diverse aquatic ecosystems spanning hundreds of kilometers of teeming estuaries and rivers. Lake Eyre itself stood 25 m deep and with a volume of some 380 cubic kilometers.

So you see a warming trend has been occurring for at least 50,000 years – not the 50 years some people would lead you to believe. And those 'concerned scientists' know this full well. It's just not in their best interests to admit it.

As we go to press on this book the climate change hysteria has reached epic proportions. Today the headlines splashed across the globe are 'Climate Change Beyond Tipping Point!' All this due to the most recent dire UN report:

New U.N. climate report offers 'bleak' emissions forecast

By Nathaniel Gronewald, E&E News Nov. 26, 2019, 9:02 AM

Global emissions are expected to keep climbing despite promises from almost 200 nations to address climate change, propelling temperatures upward and threatening to shatter the threshold of 2°C that scientists say would invite dramatic changes to ecology and the economy.

The 10th Emissions Gap Report by the United Nations Environment Program (UNEP), released today, warned that there's "no sign" greenhouse gases will hit their zenith anytime soon. It arrived a day after the World Meteorological Organization revealed record-high concentrations of carbon dioxide and other greenhouse gases in the atmosphere.

"The summary findings are bleak," the UNEP report said. "Countries collectively failed to stop the growth in global [greenhouse gas] emissions, meaning that deeper and faster cuts are now required."

The World Meteorological Organization, meanwhile, said average CO_2 concentrations in the atmosphere rose to 407.8 parts per million in 2018, surpassing its estimate in 2017 of 405.5 ppm.

UNEP's emissions gap survey, launched from Geneva, forecasts much higher greenhouse gas concentrations to come.

In the report, UNEP applauds heightened public pressure on governments to address climate change, yet laments that it's not nearly enough. The world's emissions have been increasing by about 1.5% per year for the past decade, it notes. That would lead to temperature increases of nearly 4°C by 2100, "bringing wide-ranging and destructive climate impacts."

Many media outlets represented these findings as 'beyond hope' and 'climate change has surpassed the tipping point'. Then they quickly realized their error (if climate change is beyond the tipping point then no one will care and not give them any more money) – so they trotted out some 'experts' to assure us 'things are bad, but not beyond hope'.

This saga is 'beyond' alright, it's 'beyond' a farce and into scam territory – a massive scan to get your money through tax dollars. If you're still a believer then consider what exactly these toxic greenhouses gases really are:

The primary **greenhouse gases** in Earth's atmosphere are water vapor (H_2O), carbon dioxide (CO_2), methane (CH_4), nitrous oxide (N_2O), and ozone (O_3).

Earth's atmosphere is made up of other gases essential for life and these are nitrogen (78%), oxygen (21%), and argon (0.9%). The next most common gases are carbon dioxide (0.04%), nitrous oxide, methane, and ozone. They are trace gases that account for almost one tenth of 1% of Earth's atmosphere.

Read those stats carefully:

The primary **greenhouse gases** in Earth's atmosphere are:

Water vapor (H_2O 4%) – that's WATER folks!

Carbon dioxide (CO_2 - .04%) – the bubbles in your Pepsi or Coke

Methane (CH_4 < .001%) – from cows and manure

Nitrous oxide (N_2O < .001%)

Ozone (O_3 < .001%) – smog from vehicles & factories

So the biggest offender (after water) greenhouse gas according to some esteemed scientists is CO_2. Carbon Dioxide (CO_2), largely results from natural processes like **respiration** and from the burning of fossil fuels like coal, oil and gas.

Did you catch that big cause- RESPIRATION – or better known as breathing.

The second cause of CO_2 release is deforestation, according to research published by Duke University. When trees are killed to produce goods or heat, they release the carbon that is normally stored for photosynthesis. This process releases nearly a billion tons of carbon into the atmosphere per year, according to the 2010

Global Forest Resources Assessment. Forestry and other land-use practices can offset some of these greenhouse gas emissions, according to the EPA.

Do you remember your grade school biology and science? Humans breathe in oxygen and exhale carbon dioxide.

Vegetation and trees take in the carbon dioxide and emit oxygen through photosynthesis (which requires sun light by the way).

In one day, the average person breathes out around 500 liters of the greenhouse gas CO2. So, on the face of it, we humans are a significant contributor to CO2 concentration in our atmosphere - all .04% of it. And duh, there are many more people alive today than ever in human history and far fewer trees so yeah there's bound to be an imbalance!

Now the experts can't hardly admit that people breathing are causing global warming so they come up with garbage like this statement:

'But, in reality, the CO2 we're breathing out is part of a natural cycle, by which our bodies convert carbohydrates from CO2-absorbing plants into energy, plus water and CO2. As such, we're not adding any extra CO2. In contrast, burning fossil fuels like coal releases CO2 which has been locked up for millions of years, producing a net contribution to global warming.'

That is so illogical and nobody questions it! Part of the natural cycle? How could that be when there is less vegetation and vastly more people breathing?

Furthermore we know that the total amount of atmospheric Carbon Dioxide is only 0.04% of the atmosphere. We also know that the figure for the human contribution is about 3%. That means the total human contribution from the burning of fossil fuels amounts to 0.0012%, an amount that is so tiny it is laughable.

But let's just assume that CO2 is causing global warming (we can't do anything about that pesky WATER vapor). It seems to me the answer is quite simple:

Eliminate people.

Less humans running around exhaling toxic CO2 would have all kinds of additional benefits:

There would be less farming and farm animals reducing methane.

We'd cut down fewer trees.

We'd burn less fossil fuel.

We'd drive fewer vehicles and cut smog.

Heck, a cut of about 50% would be about right. Let's cut 3.5 billion people. What a better place the earth would be!

Of course the experts and academics and scientists would never propose that – cutting the population would cut tax revenue and the government's pocketbook.

In summary, to think puny humans could actually affect earth's weather is so ludicrous it begs comparison with those in ancient times who swore the earth was the center of the universe. Boy, we are so full of ourselves!

Oh, and by the way - that UN report we mentioned stated: 'That greenhouse gases would lead to temperature increases of nearly 4°C by 2100.

You see, adults notice that year 2100, 80 years into the future and ignore the experts. And oh boy that drives them crazy and livid with anger – we're supposed to listen to scientists who know better than us.

The sad thing is now they've figured out they lost a good percentage of the adult population so they've turned to another group much easier to con: our children.

So now we have kids holding rallies and walking out of school (and they already don't spend enough time learning).

It reminds me of when I was a kid living under the threat of nuclear war and practicing air raid drills.

These so called expert climate activists are stealing our kid's childhoods and that may be the biggest crime of all.

3. Wildfires

Doing the same thing over and over is crazy, so why do we keep doing it?

I reside (can't actually say 'live') in California, unfortunately. It is one of the most mismanaged states in the union. Just look at the out of control homeless and drug addiction fueling crisis health issues and rampant crime. (California's idea to reduce crime is to just not call it a crime any longer. Do you know you have to steal over $950 to even get prosecuted?)

But if all that isn't enough to drive you crazy then we have the wildfires. Last October 2018 we had to evacuate because of a wildfire that incinerated nine miles and ended up licking literally at our front door 50 feet away. The cause, by the way, was a state government worker using road flares! How stupid can a person really be? Then to top it off, despite dozens of calls to 911 about a fire smoldering along Route 91, the fire department ignored it for

45 minutes until it was a full-fledged, out of control brush fire. So I am a little sensitive about wildfires. Our home was untouched that time, but now we live in constant anxiety during the months of October, November, and December, waiting for the next one to roar south out of the hills covered in dry brush.

The state government in California says all the wildfires are caused by global warming and this is the new normal – in other words there's nothing they can do about it. We just have to live with it. Trump is the only one calling them out on the absolute abysmal forest and wildland management brought on by our 'earth friendly environmentalists'.

Drive around California and you'll plainly see dense forests with old dead trees and vacant land from the ocean to the eastern border with brush no one ever clears or cuts. After the last few rounds of devastating wildfires the state government's lack of management can no longer be considered ignorant – it's just plain criminal stupidity.

Yes we have a dry climate – people seem to forget (remember I told you so) that Southern California was a desert. What do they expect? California doesn't get much rain, mostly due to those vast mountain ranges. SO okay, we have a dry climate don't you think a good idea would be clear away old dry brush and trees? Maybe they should quit planting incendiary palm trees everywhere. In fact palm trees should probably be illegal here.

And it's even worse in Northern California because there are even more nut cases up there impeding decisions and actions to prevent future forest fires. Not to mention they have arguably the worst utility in the entire world - PG&E. Those people are responsible for more deaths between their poorly maintained gas lines resulting in massive explosions and decrepit power lines that continually spark wild fires than any serial killer that ever lived.

But I can't do much to impact that part of the problem. What frustrates me is what happens when a wildfire inevitably starts burning. The way wildfires are fought is medieval. Throw dirt on it, throw water on it, set back fires.

Yeah, we have a few water dropping helicopters (may as well form a bucket brigade because tiny little choppers can't carry enough water to make a difference. If they could, the fires would be out fast.

And we have a few large fixed wing planes that can drop fire retardant and larger quantities of water. Unfortunately the key word here is 'few' – way too few.

Fires routinely burn thousands of acres and hundreds of square miles because 600-800 fire fighters are out there with hoses and picks and shovels like they did two hundred years ago.

Come on! Isn't it time to get serious about fighting these fires? Instead of one lone DC-10 dropping a few thousand pounds of Phos-Chek fire retardant we should have a dozen super tankers flying wing tip to wing tip dropping hundreds of thousands of gallons of water on these fires.

Make it rain!

Think that's farfetched? It just so happens the Air Force is retiring hundreds of KC-135 tankers which are each capable of carrying 23,952 gallons of water. To put this in perspective, the typical water dropping helicopter can only carry about 100 gallons. One KC-135 would be the equivalent of **239** helicopter drops!

Why not fly ten of them over a fire and drop 239,500 gallons of water. The fire would be extinguished in minutes instead of days or weeks.

So what are the drawbacks?

None that I can think of. The KC-135 is an air to air refueling tanker based on the civilian 707. It has a payload of 200,000 pounds – a gallon of water weighs 8.34 pounds FYI. I was in the Air Force for eight years and worked on KC-135s. They are reliable workhorses. Sure they require maintenance, but fixed wing aircraft are far more reliable and require far less maintenance than helicopters. Besides, the planes would only fly a few times, a few months out of the year anyway. The fact this planes could drop so much water on one pass automatically limits how often they would need to be used.

It just so happens the Air National Guard controls most of the KC-135s, so California already has KC-135 bases and personnel under the control of the governor. But that hardly matters, the Air Force is phasing out and retiring the KC-135 anyway and they'll end up mothballed in the desert. The Air Force would probably give them to the states.

Yes, the KC-135s carried jet fuel. So fill the tanks with water and fly out over the desert and dump it. Presto the fuel would be purged. The tankers would get filled with water just like they used to get filled with fuel – by tanker trucks. Water could also be pumped in directly if they were close enough to a source. Yes, the KC-135 has a boom in the tail for air to air refueling. Just remove it.

The water would be dropped over a fire by purging or dumping the tanks – the KC-135 has a dump capability in case of emergency – this would just be a normal operation going forward. The aircraft could always be retrofitted with spray nozzles if required.

Would dumping so much water be dangerous?

Answer: Is rain dangerous? I don't see any reason the KC-135s couldn't be used over residential areas – the impact of water dropping would be controlled by altitude – the higher they fly and dump, the more misty the resulting rain.

In summary I can't think of a single reason these planes wouldn't be the biggest advance in brush fire fighting ever. The only thing limiting them is lack of imagination and not thinking outside the box; of course that means it'll never happen – unless some billionaire buys one and does a demonstration for the media.

I'm rather surprised the insurance companies – who have the most to lose – don't form some consortium or association and take matters into their own hands in fighting these wildfires. There's precedent for that in the National Fire Protection Association (NFPA) and Underwriters Laboratories (UL).

Now before someone jumps down my throat for singling out California, it is true that wildfires happen in other states and around the world. While California's fire are some of the most destructive in terms of property damage and loss of life, other areas have certainly been plagued by fires variously called brush fires, forest fires, and bush fires. Fires have struck Arizona, Utah, Colorado, and even Alaska.

Bushfires and grassfires are also common throughout Australia. Bushfires are an intrinsic part of Australia's environment. Natural ecosystems have evolved with fire, and the landscape, along with its biological diversity, has been shaped by both historic and recent fires. Many of Australia's native plants are fire prone and very combustible, while numerous species depend on fire to regenerate. Indigenous Australians have long used fire as a land management tool and it continues to be used to clear land for agricultural purposes and to protect properties from intense, uncontrolled fires.

Historically, Australia's bushfires have caused loss of life and significant damage to property. While naturally occurring bushfires cannot be averted, their consequences can be minimized by implementing mitigation strategies and reducing the potential impact to areas which are most vulnerable.

In the years between 1967 and 2013, major Australian bushfires have resulted in over 8000 injuries and 433 fatalities, close to 50 per cent of all deaths from major Australian natural disasters in the period (excluding heat waves). Over this same period, bushfires cost approximately A$4.7 billion (2013 Australian dollars, including deaths and injuries but excluding most indirect losses).

Portugal has recorded one of the highest numbers of wildfires in Europe since 1993. These fires destroyed more than 10% of the country's forests and caused 18 deaths in 2003. Portugal had the highest number of forest fires in Europe in 2016, with a total of 13,261 fires.

The Amazon region made news for its raging wildfires – 90% of which were started by humans to clear areas of rain forest.

Wildfires are blamed on climate and global warming, and certainly, dry conditions are conducive to fires, but all this didn't start happening yesterday.

Way back in **1825** the Miramichi Fire in New Brunswick consumed THREE MILLION ACRES.

Okay so wildfires are bad but there are lots we can do about them.

But most importantly we need to fight them efficiently. The KC-135 water tanker could be used all over the world. Here's hoping maybe this book will get the word out.

4. Religion

Who was Mary Magdalene really?

I mentioned I was raised a Catholic. I went to a Catholic school for 12 years. I was thoroughly indoctrinated in religion. I accepted what the priests and nuns taught me and didn't think much about it.

One day while channel surfing I happened on a documentary about Mary Magdalene. I thought "Why would anyone produce a film about a prostitute who was reformed by Christ and thereafter followed him like a groupie?"

I thought that because that was what I had been taught – in religion class.

The documentary was intriguing, revealing much ambiguity in Mary of Magdala's story. Suddenly her backstory wasn't so clear as the Church portrayed it. She may have been a widower, someone Jesus cured of a disease. Faulty translations, misunderstandings, and even jealousy played into her vilification. Mary may even have not even been the woman who cleansed Christ's feet.

Later I anxiously read Dan Brown's wildly popular and controversial book 'The DaVinci Code' and learned Mary's story was even more fascinating and important – I discovered she wrote a gospel too: The Gospel of Mary.

In what is called the Gnostic gospel, Mary Magdalene appears as a disciple, singled out by Jesus for special attention. In one passage, the other disciples are discouraged and grieving Jesus' death. Mary stands up and attempts to comfort them, reminding them that Jesus' presence remains with them.

The Gospel of Mary is found in the Berlin Gnostic Codex (Papyrus Berolinensis 8502). This very important and well-preserved codex was discovered in the late-nineteenth century somewhere near Akhmim in upper Egypt. It was purchased in Cairo in 1896 by a German scholar, Dr. Carl Reinhardt, and then taken to Berlin. There is ample evidence that the Gospel of Mary was well distributed in early Christian times and existed in both an original Greek and a Coptic language translation.

This is the most complete surviving fragment of the Gospel of Mary – and it is clear this named Mary is the person we call Mary of Magdala. Two other small fragments of the Gospel of Mary from separate Greek editions were later unearthed in archaeological excavations in Egypt.

Unfortunately the surviving manuscript of the Gospel of Mary is missing pages 1 to 6 and pages 11 to 14, but no matter – the fact that the Gospel of Mary even exists and was well known at the time I was in school is pretty damning evidence against the Catholic Church. It would certainly appear the Church purposely suppressed her gospel and diminished her role as an important disciple of Jesus solely, because she was a woman.

Oh, if only I had been aware of this while I was in class – the questions I could have asked the priests! But now, all this has completely eroded any remaining faith I had in the Church. Not only did the Church do its best to outright suppress Mary Magdalene's words but it completely went against Jesus' own teachings when it came to women. Christ was one of the only men in the Bible who revered women and treated them as equals.

I believe you can blame the battle for women's rights directly on the Catholic Church. If the Catholic Church had been forthright and honest about Mary Magdalene I suspect it may not have taken 2,000 years for females to be treated as equals in society and culture.

The Discovery Channel did a fine documentary on the tradition of Mary Magdalene, with balanced commentary from several recognized scholars of early Christian and Gnostic tradition. This film is worth watching: The Secrets of Mary Magdalene.

Who was Jesus Christ really?

I believe there was a Jesus and I very much respect, admire, and adhere to his teachings.

But I don't believe he was the son of God. (It's amazing how difficult it is for me to say that, but I suppose that's what years of religious indoctrination does to you.)

I don't believe Jesus Christ was the son of God because I no longer believe in God.

Then who is the Supreme Being?

The Catholic Church (and lots of other religions) throws around the term 'Supreme Being' a lot and it is intended to refer to 'God'. I never thought much about this to be honest. I took it for granted.

Now as I look backward and inward and all around me, I realize the impact of that term and how contradictory it really is.

Supreme **Being**. God is a 'being'? How is that possible? Aren't we all beings – human beings? Does that term imply that 'God' or god is a being like us except 'supreme' [defined as: of authority or an office, or someone holding it, superior to all others]. Heck, doesn't the dictator of North Korea call himself the supreme leader?

If you met someone from a million years into the future, more technically advanced than anything we could even imagine, would that person be a supreme being?

Conversely if you went back in time a thousand years wouldn't those people of that period consider you a supreme being?

Arthur C Clark the author wrote: 'Any sufficiently advanced technology is indistinguishable from magic.' This quote sticks with me because it rings true.

Let's imagine we travel back to December 19, 1777, the Battle of Valley Forge and demonstrate a laser to George Washington. How would he react? Would he consider us a god? Probably not, but would he consider us a supreme being? Quite likely - and that's only 240 some years ago.

Now let's go back 2,000 years – and for good measure arrive in a helicopter. Now do you think we'd be viewed as a Supreme Being or god? Absolutely. We float down from the sky in a machine the likes of which no one at that time has ever imagined and couldn't even comprehend. We could give someone an aspirin or painkillers and relieve their agony. We could touch someone (give them an injection) and cure all sorts of maladies. If we were a physician we could cure practically anything: blindness (cataracts), broken bones, etc. We would undoubtedly be a god – the supreme being of the time.

I don't believe in miracles. I don't believe Jesus (or anyone else for that matter) ever performed one. There is no such thing as a miracle. These events are nothing more than erroneous perception.

Jesus could have given someone sick an aspirin and 'cured' them for all we know. Jesus could have, and probably did, use advanced technology to do all the 'miracles' in the Bible.

Jesus Christ was a supreme being but not 'God' or his son.

When I was writing my book 'Afterlife' I did a lot of research into the world's major religions. First, I had no idea there were so many:

Christianity	2.1 billion
Islam	1.6 billion
Agnostic/Atheist	≤ 1.1 billion
Hinduism	1 billion
Chinese traditional	394 million
Buddhism	376 million
Ethnic religions	300 million
African traditional	100 million
Sikhism	23 million
Juche	19 million
Spiritism	15 million
Judaism	14 million
Bahá'í	7 million
Jainism	4.2 million
Shinto	4 million
Cao Dai	4 million
Zoroastrianism	2.6 million
Tenrikyo	2 million
Neo-Paganism	1 million
Unitarian	800,000
Rastafarianism	600,000

Scientology   500,000

Then I was struck by the similarities of all of them.

Almost every one had a prophet.

Why were so many prophets the same?

Why are there different religions for different people if there is only one 'God'?

What follows is a fictional account of the trial of Jack, the fourth prophet, and leaders of the world's religions, from my novel 'Afterlife', which illustrates my ideas on this matter:

"I know who you are. I know you all. You are the usurpers of the Creator's authority." Jack announced dramatically.

The stunned holy men looked at one another with jaws dropped. Only Rabbi Goldbaum managed to retain a semblance of composure. "My boy, you are on very, very dangerous ground. Perhaps you should explain yourself before the Council's honor is irreparably harmed and you are in too deep to extricate yourself!"

"I have a message for you from He who I come in the name of..." Jack began.

"You do claim to come from God!" the Ayatollah shouted an accusation.

"He prefers to be called 'The Creator'. Gods are just figments of men's imaginations."

"So you claim to be God's Son then, speaking for Him?" the Cardinal demanded when he regained his breath.

"I am not God's son. I am not a prophet nor the messiah..."

"Then you are the Antichrist, the false messiah!" Cardinal Mendez cut Jack off this time.

"There is no Antichrist. I am The Creator's messenger."

"Are you saying there is no evil?" Manoj Gupta, the Hindu holy man asked, clearly curious.

"There can be no good without evil. Like matter and anti-matter, everything has a positive and negative. It's a basic tenet of the Creator's Universe."

"Is there Satan then?" Manoj Gupta wanted clarification.

"No. There is no Satan or devil and there is no hell. Those are things made up by you, by men, to frighten your followers and little children." Jack spat out.

"You are bordering on blasphemy! The Antichrist is the representative of the Devil himself," the Cardinal maintained.

"Your own words speak volumes of your arrogance. No one else among you believes in such a figure, only so-called 'Christians'. You each have variations of your 'religions' to suit yourselves. How can there be more than one version of His words?"

Ramares was struck by what Jack said and sat up in rapt attention. It was something he always wondered himself. *How can God be different for different men? It made no sense.*

"Then is there a heaven, paradise, an afterlife?" the Hindu holy man asked again.

"Yes, but not the one someone so clumsily portrayed to trick the people. If you live a good life your essence, your 'soul', goes to The Creator's place of eternal happiness," Jack told them.

"And if you are evil?" the Hindu had to ask.

"You cease to exist and your essence is recycled into dirt for The Creator's projects."

"How dare you come before this holy body and tell us what to believe?" the Cardinal shouted.

"How can you each believe something different? How can you each claim yours is the one true god? There is only one Creator. There is not a different Creator for white men and black men and Asians, or Jews."

"What you say *is* blasphemy!" the Ayatollah shouted above the increasing din.

"Here we go again," Jack said with a pronounced sigh.

"And you are anti-Semitic, lumping Judaism in with Christianity," the Rabbi was incensed now too.

Jack laughed out loud at this. "There is but one Creator, and one version of His rules for life: Treat others as you want to be treated and live your life with a good heart. That's it, it's simple," Jack told them in a commanding voice. "You all have invented your religions and rules to suit yourselves and make your followers obey you and give you money. You are the worst kind of slave masters. And you have murdered so many of your fellow men in the name of your false religions." Jack's words were too much for some of the holy men.

"If you claim to be from God then ask Him to strike down this proceeding!" Cardinal Mendez was livid.

"You are so arrogant as to assume The Creator would waste time on this tiny insignificant little world? How can you be so conceited as to think you are the only of His people? There are quadrillions of beings in The Creator's Universe. Frankly homo sapiens are rather trivial," Jack came close to sneering.

"If you claim to be from God then *you* show us a sign!" the Rabbi demanded.

"You require your followers to have faith and believe sight unseen, but you do not believe unless you are shown? What hypocrites!" Jack shot back.

"This man is truly psychotic!" the Cardinal exclaimed.

"I am not insane. You want signs? Look around you. This world is falling apart and will cease to exist soon. Instead of coming together as one world, one human race, you continue to be segregated with different languages! But you so called holy leaders selfishly maintain your individuality and force your faithful to blindly follow. Instead of coming together you force your people apart. You outright lie to your people. Not one of The Creator's other worlds is in such dire straights."

"This is some sort of joke!" Rabbi Goldbaum shouted.

"If you are not insane, then you are possessed by the very devil you claim doesn't exist. I move we close these proceedings and take a vote on this blasphemer's fate," Cardinal Mendez slammed the table with the palm of his hand.

"I second that! I vote for execution!" the Ayatollah roared...

"You are fools", Jack replied. "Siddhartha Gautama, the Buddha was The Creator's first messenger in 563 BCE. He visited the most advanced race at the time the Asians. The Creator had high hopes The Buddha would prevail but Asia remained in isolation as the Roman Empire expanded. So He sent Jesus Christ 563 years later in 0 CE, the Common Era. Once again man had an opportunity to unite under Christ's message and the unified Roman rule. But humanity fragmented again so He sent Abū al-Qāsim Muhammad 570 years later, with the exact same message, alarmed that religions had began fighting each other. And now I am Jack, The Creator's fourth and final messenger."

Isn't it curious that the 'prophets' or 'messiahs' arrived when they did?

The Buddha in 563 BC.

Christ in 0 BC

Muhammad in 570 AD

Are we past due for another one? Has one come and gone without notice? Well there are certainly plenty who claimed to be prophets or messiahs and it makes for some interesting reading:

Jewish messiah claimants

Simon bar Kokhba (died c. 135), founded a short-lived Jewish state before being defeated in the Second Jewish-Roman War.

Moses of Crete, who in about 440–470 persuaded the Jews of Crete to walk into the sea, as Moses had done, to return to Israel. The results were disastrous and he soon disappeared.

Ishak ben Ya'kub Obadiah Abu 'Isa al-Isfahani (684–705), who led a revolt in Persia against the Umayyad Caliph 'Abd al-Malik ibn Marwan.

David Alroy, born in Kurdistan, who around 1160 agitated against the caliph before being assassinated.

Moses Botarel of Cisneros, active around 1413; claimed to be a sorcerer able to combine the names of God.

Asher Lämmlein, a German near Venice who proclaimed himself a forerunner of the Messiah in 1502.

David Reubeni (1490–1541?) and **Solomon Molcho** (1500–1532), messianic adventurers who travelled in Portugal, Italy and Turkey; Molcho, who was a baptised Catholic, was tried by the Inquisition, convicted of apostasy and burned at the stake.

Sabbatai Zevi (1626–1676), an Ottoman Jew who claimed to be the Messiah, but then converted to Islam; still has followers today in the Dönmeh.

Jacob Querido (?–1690), claimed to be the new incarnation of Sabbatai; later converted to Islam and led the Dönmeh.

Miguel Cardoso (1630–1706), another successor of Sabbatai who claimed to be the "Messiah ben Ephraim".

Löbele Prossnitz (?–1750), attained some following amongst former followers of Sabbatai, calling himself the "Messiah ben Joseph".

Jacob Joseph Frank (1726–1791), who claimed to be the reincarnation of King David and preached a synthesis of Christianity and Judaism.

Yosef Yitzchak Schneersohn (r. 1920 - 1950), sixth rebbe (spiritual leader) of Chabad Lubavitch, claimed to be the Messiah.

Menachem Mendel Schneerson (1902–1994), seventh rebbe of Chabad Lubavitch, claimed to be the Messiah by his followers.

Christian messiah claimants

Simon Magus (early 1st century), was a Samaritan, and a native of Gitta; he was considered a god in Simonianism; he "darkly hinted" that he himself was Christ, calling himself the Standing One.

Dositheos the Samaritan (mid 1st century), was one of the supposed founders of Mandaeanism. Dositheus pretended to be the Christ (Messiah), applying Deuteronomy 18:15 to himself.

Tanchelm of Antwerp (c. 1110), who violently opposed the sacrament and the Eucharist.

Ann Lee (1736–1784), a central figure to the Shakers, who thought she "embodied all the perfections of God" in female form and considered herself to be Christ's female counterpart in 1772.

Bernhard Müller (c. 1799–1834) claimed to be the Lion of Judah and a prophet in possession of the Philosopher's stone.

John Nichols Thom (1799–1838), who had achieved fame and followers as Sir William Courtenay and adopted the claim of Messiah after a period in a mental institute.

Arnold Potter (1804–1872), Latter Day Saint schismatic leader; called himself "Potter Christ"

Hong Xiuquan (1814–1864), Hakka Chinese; claimed himself to be the younger brother of Jesus Christ; started the Taiping Rebellion and founded the Heavenly Kingdom of Great Peace. Committed suicide before the fall of Tianjing (Nanjing) in 1864.

Mirza Husayn 'Ali Nuri, Bahá'u'lláh (1817–1892), born Shiite, adopting Bábism in 1844 (see "Bab" in Muslim messiah claimants section below). In 1863, he claimed to be the promised one of all religions, and founded the Bahá'í Faith.

Jacobina Mentz Maurer (1841 or 1842–1874) was a German-Brazilian woman who lived and died in the state of Rio Grande do Sul who emerged as a messianic prophetess, a representation of God, and later declared the very reincarnation of Jesus Christ on earth by her German-speaking community called Die Muckers (or the false saints) by her enemies, Die Spotters (or the mockers). After a number of deadly confrontations with outsiders, Jacobina was shot to death together with many of her followers by the Brazilian Imperial Army.

William W. Davies (1833–1906), Latter Day Saint (Mormon) schismatic leader; claimed that his infant son Arthur (born 1868) was the reincarnated Jesus Christ.

Cyrus Reed Teed (October 18, 1839 – December 22, 1908, erroneously Cyrus Tweed) was a U.S. eclectic physician and alchemist turned religious leader and messiah. In 1869, claiming divine inspiration, Dr. Teed took on the name Koresh and proposed a new set of scientific and religious ideas he called Koreshanity.

Abd-ru-shin (18 April 1875 – 6 December 1941), founder of the Grail Movement.

Lou de Palingboer (Louwrens Voorthuijzen)[26] (1898-1968), a dutch charismatic leader who claimed to be god and the messiah from 1950 until his death in 1968.

Father Divine (George Baker) (c. 1880 –1965), an African American spiritual leader from about 1907 until his death who claimed to be God.

André Matsoua (1899–1942), Congolese founder of Amicale, proponents of which subsequently adopted him as Messiah in the late 1920s.

Samael Aun Weor (1917–1977), born Víctor Manuel Gómez Rodríguez, Colombian citizen and later Mexican, was an author, lecturer and founder of the 'Universal Christian Gnostic Movement', according to him, 'the most powerful movement ever founded'. By 1972, he referenced that his death and resurrection would be occurring before 1978.

Ahn Sahng-hong (1918–1985), founder of the World Mission Society Church of God and worshiped by the members as the messiah.

Sun Myung Moon (1920–2012), founder and leader of the Unification Church established in Seoul, South Korea, who considered himself the Second Coming of Christ, but not Jesus himself. Although it is generally believed by Unification Church members ("Moonies") that he was the Messiah and the Second Coming of Christ.

Yahweh ben Yahweh (1935–2007), born as **Hulon Mitchell, Jr.,** a black nationalist and separatist who created the Nation of Yahweh and allegedly orchestrated the murder of dozens of persons.

Laszlo Toth (1940–2012) claimed he was Jesus Christ as he battered Michelangelo's Pieta with a geologist hammer.

Wayne Bent (born 1941), also known as **Michael Travesser** of the Lord Our Righteousness Church, also known as the "Strong City Cult", convicted December 15, 2008 of one count of criminal sexual contact of a minor.

Iesu Matayoshi (born 1944), in 1997 he established the World Economic Community Party based on his conviction that he is God and the Christ.

Jung Myung Seok (born 1945), a South Korean who was a member of the Unification Church in the 1970s, before breaking off to found the dissenting group now known as Providence Church in 1980. He also considers himself the Second Coming of Christ, but not Jesus.

Claude Vorilhon now known as Raël "messenger of the Elohim" (born 1946), a French professional test driver and former car journalist became founder and leader of UFO religion the Raël Movement in 1972, which teaches that life on Earth was scientifically created by a species of extraterrestrials, which they call Elohim. He claimed he met an extraterrestrial humanoid in 1973 and became the Messiah.

José Luis de Jesús (1946–2013), founder and leader of Creciendo en Gracia sect (Growing In Grace International Ministry, Inc.), based in Miami, Florida. He claimed to be both Jesus Christ returned and the Antichrist, and exhibited a "666" tattoo on his forearm. He has referred to himself as Jesucristo Hombre, which translates to "Jesus Christ made Man".

Inri Cristo (born 1948) of Indaial, Brazil, a claimant to be the second Jesus.

Apollo Quiboloy (born 1950), founder and leader of the Kingdom of Jesus Christ religious group, who claims that Jesus Christ is the "Almighty Father," that Quiboloy is "His Appointed Son," and that salvation is now completed. Proclaims himself as the "Appointed Son of the God".

David Icke (born 1952), of Great Britain, has described himself as "the son of God", and a "channel for the Christ spirit".

Brian David Mitchell was born on October 18, 1953 in Salt Lake City, Utah, he believed himself the fore-ordained angel born on earth to be the Davidic "servant" prepared by God.

David Koresh (Vernon Wayne Howell) (1959–1993), leader of the Branch Davidians. (See Waco, Texas)

Maria Devi Christos (born 1960), founder of the Great White Brotherhood.

Sergey Torop (born 1961), who started to call himself "Vissarion", founder of the Church of the Last Testament and the spiritual community Ecopolis Tiberkul in Southern Siberia.

Alan John Miller (born 1962), founder of Divine Truth, a new religious movement based in Australia. Alan John Miller, also known as A.J., who claims to be Jesus of Nazareth through reincarnation. Miller was formerly an elder in the Jehovah's Witnesses.

David Shayler (born 1965), former MI5 agent and whistleblower who declared himself the Messiah on 7 July 2007.

Muslim messiah claimants

Muhammad Jaunpuri (1443–1505), who traveled Northeastern India; he influenced the Mahdavia and the Zikris.

Báb (1819–1850), who declared himself to be the promised Mahdi in Shiraz, Iran in 1844. (Related to Baha'i claims--see the Christian

Messiah Claimants section above--Mirza Husayn 'Ali Nuri, also known as Baha'u'llah.)

Muhammad Ahmad ("The Mad Mahdi") (1844–1885), who declared himself the Mahdi in 1881, defeated the Ottoman Egyptian authority, and founded the Mahdist Sudan.

Mirza Ghulam Ahmad of Qadian, India (1835–1908), proclaimed himself to be both the expected Mahdi and Messiah, being the only person in Islamic history who claimed to be both. Crucially, however, he claimed that Jesus had died a natural death after surviving crucifixion, and that prophecies concerning his future advent referred to the Mahdi himself bearing the qualities and character of Jesus rather than to his physical return alongside the Mahdi. He founded the Ahmadiyya Movement in 1889 envisioning it to be the rejuvenation of Islam.

Sayyid Mohammed Abdullah Hassan (1864–1920), who led the Dervish State in present-day Somalia in a two-decade long resistance movement between 1900 and 1920.

Rashad Khalifa (1935–1990), an Egyptian-American biochemist who claimed that he had discovered a mathematical code in the text of the Qur'an involving the number 19; he later claimed to be the "Messenger of the Covenant" and founded the "Submitters International" movement before being murdered.

Juhayman al-Otaybi (1936–1980), who seized the Grand Mosque in Mecca in November 1979 and declared his son-in-law the Mahdi.

Louis Farrakhan (May 11, 1933) Nation of Islam leader on 04/04/2019, claims to be Jesus in 'Saviours' Day' address: 'I am the Messiah'

Hasan Mezarci (May 11, 1954) Conservative Islamist politician and member of parliament in Republic of Turkey (1991-1995), was expelled from Refah party and imprisoned for his extreme view against Secularism. He claimed to be the Messiah during his imprisonment.

Harun Yahya (February 2, 1956) leader of Islamic creationist cult leader, Active in Turkey since 1980, He believes himself to be the Messiah and focuses his brand of Islam on close reading of the Quran, with dramatic presentations similar to Christian televangelism. and the author of The Atlas of Creation.

Other or combination messiah claimants

Emperor Haile Selassie I of Ethiopia (1892–1975), Messiah of the Rastafari movement. Never claimed himself to be Messiah, but was thus proclaimed by Leonard Howell, amongst others.

André Matsoua (1899–1942), Congolese founder of Amicale, proponents of which subsequently adopted him as Messiah.

Samael Aun Weor (1917–1977), born Víctor Manuel Gómez Rodríguez, Colombian citizen and later Mexican, was an author, lecturer and founder of the Universal Christian Gnostic Movement. By 1972, Samael Aun Weor referenced that his death and resurrection would be occurring before 1978.

Nirmala Srivastava (1923–2011), guru and goddess of Sahaja Yoga, proclaimed herself to be the Comforter promised by Jesus (that is, the incarnation of the Holy Ghost / Adi Shakti).

Jose Luis de Jesus Miranda (born 1946 – died 2013), a Puerto Rican preacher who had claimed to be both "the Man Jesus Christ" and the Antichrist at the same time. He claimed he was indwelled with the same spirit that dwelled in Jesus, however, Miranda also contradicted his claims of being Christ incarnate by also claiming he was the Antichrist, even going as far as tattooing the number of the beast (666) on his forearm, a behavior his followers also adopted. Founder of the "Growing in Grace" ministries, Miranda died on August 14, 2013 due to liver cancer.

Riaz Ahmed Gohar Shahi (born 25 November 1941) is a spiritual leader and the founder of the spiritual movements Messiah Foundation International (MFI) and Anjuman Serfaroshan-e-Islam. He is controversial for being declared the Mehdi, Messiah, and Kalki Avatar by the MFI.

Raël, founder and leader of Raëlism (born 30 September 1946); Rael claimed he met an extraterrestrial being in 1973 and became the Messiah.

World Teacher (unknown), a being claimed to be the Theosophical Maitreya and the Messiah (promised one) of all religions. He is said to have descended from the higher planes and manifested a physical body in early 1977 in the Himalayas, then on 19 July 1977 he is said to have taken a commercial airplane flight from Pakistan to England. He is currently said to be living in secret in London.

Ryuho Okawa (born 7 July 1956), is the founder of Happy Science in Japan. Okawa claims to channel the spirits of Muhammad, Christ, Buddha and Confucius and claims to be the incarnation of the supreme spiritual being called El Cantare.

Was one of these people another messiah?

Where did 'life' come from?

I stated earlier that I don't believe in 'God'; however 'life' came from somewhere. We spoke previously of evolution, but where did it all start? Science would have us believe all life somehow spontaneously sprang into being from a perfect mix of climate, chemicals, and lightning.

That makes no sense when you examine 'life' closely. The odds of even one single cell forming out of random substances and other factors is beyond astronomical.

The simplest form of life, a single cell amoeba, contains 15,727 genes that code for proteins, compared to about 23,000 in humans. With those genes, the organism can eat and reproduce, crawl or swim, live with or without oxygen, and organize itself internally much as a human cell does.

The protozoa Amoeba dubia genome has 670 billion units of DNA, or base pairs. The genome of a cousin, Amoeba proteus, has a mere 290 billion base pairs, making it 100 times larger than the human genome.

Let that sink in for a few seconds. Forget about comparisons to humans; let's just consider the earth back at the beginning when there was no life. Somehow BILLIONS of bits of DNA randomly formed perfectly and aligned in a single cell organism? That makes no sense and defies all logic.

Even more astounding is what had to have happened after that single cell formed. Somehow all that complex RNA and DNA had to split and reproduce, forming a new complex single cell. Then those two cells have to split. Eventually, somehow, those single cells had to merge and form the next even more complex creature like maybe a worm. Okay, even if that were possible what happened next? How did the worm reproduce? You mean somehow two worms formed randomly out of a bunch of clinging single cells?

The biologists never seem to get around to explaining how two of any forms of life emerged <u>at the same time</u> so they could reproduce. Sure there are organisms that can reproduce themselves but at some point as the next higher order creature forms it has to have a mate – and that means the astronomical odds against one life forming are now doubled!

Science knows the astronomical odds against this theory of how life started and marvels at it but doesn't want anyone to examine it too closely because how absurd it sounds. Religion loves how impossible this sounds because it points to a god.

Now let's look at life today as we know it and are familiar with it. Every living thing has a purpose. Every organism has built in instructions and instinct for survival and reproduction. Even insects spend all of their time hunting for food, preparing a home (nest), attracting a mate, and reproducing. The extremes some creatures go to in order to mate are mind boggling. Most color in nature has the sole purpose of attracting mates.

Life on earth is in harmony. Plants drop seeds, flowers attract bees, and insects eat each other and keep their populations in check – as do many mammals. If humans stay out of things and don't meddle, mostly every living thing keeps in balance.

Nothing in nature is random; every living thing has a purpose. Nature is too perfect, too well organized to have randomly evolved from single cell formed out of chemicals and lightning.

Common sense and logic point to a Creator, a Supreme Being who likely experiments with life for fun or as a hobby. The Creator is not a god. The Creator probably sits in a lab somewhere in the universe or even in another dimension and fiddles with the building blocks of life and then seeds planets with his creations. The Creator cares little about his creations, he or she or it doesn't have time. They probably check on progress once in a while and then go on to the next experiment or project.

Maybe the Creator did send some representatives - The Buddha in 563 BC, Christ in 0 BC, and Muhammad in 570 AD, down here to earth to put us back on track. We didn't listen to any of them so the Creator gave up and moved on.

The Creator has to be billions of years old – older than the universe. Perhaps there is a race of Creators whose sole function is to create life. Maybe the Creator is not a being but an entity of pure energy.

The notion of a creator makes as much sense – or even more so – than life spontaneously formed from a lightning strike in the ocean.

Of course this theory begs the question:

Who created the Creator?

Ah, the great paradox of all religions. There is no answer.

We do not understand the universe. Our brains are as yet too small to comprehend its vastness or what secrets it hides. I imagine the answer is out there. We don't even know what makes up most of the universe. Physicists call it 'Dark Matter' but have no idea what it really is.

Perhaps the Creator just always existed and always will. The first law of thermodynamics, also known as Law of Conservation of Energy, states that energy can neither be created nor destroyed; energy can only be transferred or changed from one form to another. This would infer the Creator is a pure energy being who always *was*.

Do we really have souls?

The weight of the soul

During my research I ran across a most fascinating experiment concerning the 'soul'.

The 21 grams experiment refers to a scientific study published in 1907 by Duncan MacDougall, a physician from Haverhill, Massachusetts. MacDougall hypothesized that souls have physical weight, and attempted to measure the mass lost by a human when the soul departed the body. MacDougall attempted to measure the mass change of six patients at the moment of death. One of the six subjects lost three-fourths of an ounce (21.3 grams).

MacDougall stated his experiment would have to be repeated many times before any conclusion could be obtained. The experiment is widely regarded as flawed and unscientific due to the small sample size, the methods used, as well as the fact only one of the six subjects met the hypothesis. The case has been cited as an example of selective reporting. Despite its rejection within the scientific community, MacDougall's experiment popularized the concept that the soul has weight, and specifically that it weighs 21 grams.

In 1901, Duncan MacDougall, a physician from Haverhill, Massachusetts, who wished to scientifically determine if a soul had weight, identified six patients in nursing homes whose deaths were imminent. Four were suffering from tuberculosis, one from diabetes, and one from unspecified causes. MacDougall specifically chose people who were suffering from conditions that caused physical exhaustion, as he needed the patients to remain still when they died to measure them accurately. When the patients looked like they were close to death, their entire bed was placed on an industrial sized scale that was sensitive within two tenths of an ounce (5.6 grams).

One of the patients lost weight but then put the weight back on, and two of the other patients registered a loss of weight at death but a few minutes later lost even more weight. One of the patients lost three-fourths of an ounce or 21.3 grams in weight, coinciding with the time of death. MacDougall disregarded the results of another patient on the grounds the scales were "not finely adjusted", and discounted the results of another as the patient died while the equipment was still being calibrated. On the belief that humans have souls and that animals do not, MacDougall later measured the changes in weight from fifteen dogs after death. MacDougall reported that none of the dogs lost any weight after death.

While MacDougall believed that the results from his experiment showed the human soul might have weight, his report, which was not published until 1907, stated the experiment would have to be repeated many times before any conclusion could be obtained.

The experiment was never repeated or if it was, it was never reported. And I doubt anyone would attempt it due to the ramifications from all sides.

This is so fascinating not only for what it purported to show but also because it's practically the definition of a 'hot potato'. If the results were duplicated and prove the soul has weight just imagine the uproar from the scientific community. If no weight difference were found the religious community would condemn it.

The experiment is so simple to perform it could easily have been duplicated. I suspect someone has and the results will be suppressed forever.

The real answer is probably if we do have 'souls' they are pure energy 'life force' and therefore virtually impossible to weigh. It may very well be possible to measure energy escaping or leaving body upon death.

I'm sure though such an experiment would be entirely too controversial.

If we do have a life force energy or soul – and energy cannot be destroyed, then it is quite possible our souls do 'live on' forever. Maybe reincarnation is not as farfetched as it sounds.

5. Government

Why are humans seemingly destined to repeat our mistakes?

We just can't seem to remember the past. Our collective memory is so short it's surprising we managed to survive this long.

Despite decades of complete and utter failure in China, Russia, Cuba, and lately Venezuela, socialism and communism are in vogue again – in the United States of all places! And this is while Russia and China are exploring capitalism.

Socialism and communism: Free housing, free education, free food, free healthcare - where do I sign up?

I knew people were shallow, but this trend is too much.

Socialism and communism are the refuge of the lazy and it appears we've managed to raise generations of lazy people. That's the only explanation for this desire to elect people who will provide everything you want for free.

I'm all for free education and free health care for all, but somehow it has to be paid for. Ask yourself: are the professors and teachers and doctors going to work for free? If there's one eternal truth it's that 'you get what you pay for'.

Pay nothing (or very little) and you'll get nothing. Do you really want to go to a doctor for a life threatening illness who is making $10 - $20 an hour? Would you trust your kids to teachers making minimum wage?

Oh, you would pay doctors more? Who decides what that would be?

Well if higher education were free then doctors wouldn't need to be paid more to cover their education - right? Except those medical schools and professors have to get paid too.

Is the present system perfect?

No, capitalism is flawed by greed.

There is too much money in the hands of too few. That is absolutely true. Does anyone really need more than a billion dollars? No, not hardly.

Some people say if you collect all the money in existence all over the world and redistributed it equitably you could pay for education, housing, food, and health care for all. So let's have some fun and figure it out logically:

When money is considered as the physical coins, bank notes, and the ones deposited in both checking and savings accounts; the total amount globally is approximately $36.8 trillion. However, when this physical money includes the ones held in the accessible accounts, the amount rises to roughly $90.4 trillion. May 20, 2018

https://www.worldatlas.com/www.worldatlas.com › articles › how-much-money-is-there-in-the-world

How Much Money Is There in the World? - WorldAtlas.com

The current world population is 7.7 billion as of November 2019 according to the most recent United Nations estimates elaborated by Worldometers. The term "World Population" refers to the human population (the total number of humans currently living) of the world.

https://www.worldometers.info/www.worldometers.info › world-population

World Population Clock: 7.7 Billion People (2019)

The math is simple. We'll round it off:

$90 trillion divided by 8 billion = $11,250 each.

Is that really true? That's it, a measly $11,250 each?

Hmmm, not much you're going to do with eleven thousand dollars is there? How does that wealth redistribution and socialism work again?

And what all these loonies fail to understand is once you distribute all that money – that's it, there is no more. The world economy would collapse because no one would be producing anything.

Economics states that the value of any good is determined by its supply and demand and the supply and demand for other goods in the economy. A price for any good is the amount of money it takes to get that good. Inflation occurs when the price of goods increases—in other words when money becomes less valuable relative to those other goods.

While that may be true, people must have the means of acquiring those goods or services and the only two methods are barter and money.

Money represents value and value comes from producing or rarity (gold, diamonds, etc.).

Someone invents something, workers produce it, and the inventor sells it to other workers and pays his workers. It's basically that simple.

If no one has incentive to invent products or grow food or mine minerals no value will be produced and we will all starve in the dark and cold.

At first glance it seems very benevolent to give people free housing, free food, free education, and free health care, but execution is nearly impossible. Socialism and Communism require all sorts of compromises and no one ends up happy or satisfied.

Let's examine just one facet of 'free for all': healthcare.

Medicare accounts for a significant portion of federal spending. In FY 2018, the Medicare program cost $582 billion — about 14 percent of total federal government spending. After Social Security, Medicare was the second largest program in the federal budget last year. Apr 30, 2019

Currently, 44 million beneficiaries— only 15 percent of the U.S. population—are enrolled in the Medicare program.

The current population of the United States of America is 329,784,810 as of Thursday, November 14, 2019, based on Worldometers elaboration of the latest United Nations data.

So to provide Medicare-like healthcare to all 330 million people in the U.S. we would be talking something like:

330 million/ 44 million = 7.5 X $582 billion = $ 4,365,000,000,000 per year.

That's $4.3 trillion every year.

The total annual tax revenue from all sources is about $3.6 trillion.

Obviously healthcare for all will cost $7 billion more than the federal government brings in.

And that doesn't include free housing, free food, or free education. It also doesn't include little things like defense, infrastructure, social security, and about a thousand other things the feds pay for.

Okay then, let's just provide free healthcare and forgive all student debt.

As of 2018, a total of 44.2 Million borrowers now owe a total of over $1.5 Trillion in student debt.

So now we're on the hook for $1.5 trillion in student loans and $4.3 trillion for healthcare. That's only $5.8 trillion.

So we'll just raise taxes – by 62% - Bill Gates and Jeff Bezos can pay for it, but that still wouldn't cover a quarter of the federal budget.

During FY2018, the federal government spent $4.11 trillion, up $127 billion or 3.2% vs. FY2017 spending of $3.99 trillion. Spending increased for all major categories and was mainly driven by higher spending for Social Security, net interest on the debt, and defense.

If we forgave student debt and paid for healthcare for all, the new federal budget would be: $4.11 + $4.3 + $1.5 = $9.91 trillion.

$9.91 trillion!

Or look at it another way: $9.91 trillion / 330 million people =

$30,030.30 for every man, woman, and child in the United States.

See how all this is just a pipe dream?

I can think of only one manner in which a society could provide 'free for all' to its citizens:

Robots and Artificial Intelligence

Robots, controlled and managed by AI, would perform all labor and work.

Robots would plant seeds, maintain and harvest the crops and transport them to distribution.

Robots would teach all levels of education.

Robots would perform all medical care.

Once the robots were manufactured and paid for there would be little cost. Robots would manufacture themselves eventually. At that point humans would not need to do anything. Everything would be free.

Oh, wait a minute, we're frightened to death of robots and Artificial Intelligence!

'Concerned scientists' shout through the media every day how dangerous robots and AI are.

Gee, does that sound familiar?

This brings me to the main point of this section:

Unintended Consequences

The fatal flaw of humans: we are unable to see the consequences of our actions.

The term 'unintended' is of course a complete cop out excuse. There is really no such thing as unintended. There are only consequences which we didn't think through.

For some reason humans are absolutely unable to see the consequences of our actions.

We drive a car while drunk or high.

We steal knowing full well either the victim is going to get even or we will be caught sooner or later.

We have affairs knowing full well we'll ruin our lives and our children.

We have children without being able to or wanting to raise them.

We murder knowing we will probably, sooner or later, get locked up for a long time.

We don't clear brush and dead trees and wring our hands when fires sweep through neighborhoods destroying people's homes and lives.

We dump toxic chemicals into our own water supply.

We don't maintain our infrastructure: roads, power lines, bridges and watch as people die.

We don't adequately fund police or fire departments and wonder why crime and wildfires are out of control.

Again, it begs the question:

How stupid are we?

Stupid enough to drive around high as a kite, with no license or insurance, in a car with broken tail lights and loaded with drugs in plain sight, just waiting for a cop to pull us over.

One of my most favorite stupid crimes is the Ponzi Scheme.

A Ponzi scheme is an investment fraud that pays existing investors with funds collected from new investors. Ponzi scheme organizers often promise to invest your money and generate high returns with little or no risk. But in many Ponzi schemes, the fraudsters do not invest the money – they keep it and use it to buy mansions, luxury cars, and exotic vacations.

Now unless you're planning to leave the planet, you are almost certain to be caught. Inevitably one of the later investors will demand their return but since you spent the money, there's nothing to give them.

But people still do it - and they lie, steal, cheat, and murder...

The fatal flaw of humans is we are unable to see the consequences of our actions. This likely is a part of our overall violent tendencies.

Governments are supposed to protect us from ourselves. Governments make laws prohibiting such activity which will result in unpleasant consequences.

Unfortunately governments are comprised of humans – the same people who can't foresee the consequences of their actions.

Governments are some of the worst when it comes to being unable to foresee the consequences of their actions. And in this way ALL governments are deeply flawed no matter whether they are based on democracy, socialism, communism, capitalism, or monarchy, or dictatorship.

The only mechanism that will really save us from ourselves is when we are finally ruled by Artificial Intelligence.

Sorry, that's just the way it is. Humans are never going to change – that much is obvious after thousands of years.

6. The Wonderful Business World

I started this little treatise with an anecdote about how my mind was opened in the corporate world so it seems appropriate to close with a discussion on business. And besides since almost everyone has a job and a majority work for some business or other, there is information many of you can use to your advantage.

The other reason I'm mentioning this subject is because if there's any area of human society that needs questioning, it's the business world. I spent over 50 years working in almost all aspects of business – from delivering newspapers, to security guard, to manager, director, and vice president. About 75% of my work experience was with companies that serviced everything from individual homeowners to Fortune 100 corporations and all levels of government. As such I was exposed to virtually every type of consumer and every conceivable type of business.

I will warn you that questioning business practices won't make you popular but eventually (especially if you uncover dumb things going on) it will get you noticed and maybe promoted.

Now if there's one phrase I've heard most often in every business I ever came into contact with, it's this:

"That's the way we've always done it."

The instant you hear this in response to a question, you can be 99% certain it's something stupid.

For example, at one location I noticed our delivery trucks weren't getting on the road until after nine am, despite a 7:30 am starting time for the employees. Of course I know people waste time in the morning but this was a little outrageous. The next morning I went in early and learned the reason for the delay: all the delivery trucks were parked hundreds of feet away from the loading dock. Every morning the drivers had to move their trucks one at a time to the one loading dock, get loaded, and finally leave. The last truck didn't get out until almost nine am and I could see why.

When I inquired about this procedure I got the above answer: 'That's the way we've always done it.'

I pressed the issue and asked an old timer why.

It turned out, many years prior, the boss's brother in law used to park his personal car near the dock because he didn't want to walk far. One day his car got dented and he blamed one of the delivery drivers. From that day on all trucks had to be parked far away – costing the company untold thousands in wasted man-hours and upset customers who didn't get their deliveries until late in the morning.

In another situation I noticed a lot of service calls being held over for days. Service calls are a huge expense for companies – whether the customer pays for them or not – and most of ours had service agreements so they paid a flat annual fee. To roll a service technician out costs:

Salary (travel time, traffic jams, and actual work)

Fuel

Insurance

Vehicle maintenance - wear & tear

Exposure to accidents & potential liability

When I investigated further I discovered in most of these held over open status service calls, a service tech had already been out once. That made the problem twice as bad because now each one represented two visits.

When I dug further I found every one was on hold for parts. A service tech went out, found they needed a part to fix it, and had to go back to the office to pick one up. Since they all had prescheduled calls for the entire day they didn't get back to replace the part until days later.

So not only was the company paying for two trips but our customers were upset because their security system was down for days.

When I learned the average cost of the parts was less than $100 (and in most cases $35-$40), I was livid.

Of course, *that's the way we've always done it.*

Some manager, way back when, was afraid his inventory was too high so he forbid keeping anything in stock. Businesses are often very big on 'false economy' – they save a dollar and cost themselves hundreds.

The simple solution was to stock the most commonly needed parts on every truck.

Problem solved, money saved, customers happy.

So any time someone tells you: **"That's the way we've always done it" – question it!**

I thought I'd share my basic tenets when it comes to business:

Customer satisfaction is nearly impossible to measure

All workers have a default level of production

Sales is one of the most important departments

Every report you see will be wrong in some regard

Most companies are improperly billed

Most company's invoices are wrong

Most companies are woefully inefficient

The CEO or president needs to lead

Customer Satisfaction

I have news for all you owners, presidents, directors, and CEOs: **Customers are not loyal, they are lazy.**

No matter what you think or what you measured, or what statistics you think you have, there is no such thing as customer loyalty. Oh you might produce reports that claim you have 81.7% customer retention, but that's bogus and will evaporate into thin air under certain circumstances.

Customers only stay with you because they are generally too lazy to change. It's too much trouble and hassle to change suppliers, vendors, contractors, or whatever role you fill in their business or lives.

While this is good at first glance, it is a two edged sword however. As soon as a competitor comes around with cheaper prices, better service, and a hassle free way of doing business with them, your customers will drop you like yesterday's news.

Once you understand this, you can plan and institute methods to avoid losing customers as much as possible.

First – you must be perfect. Your business must deliver 100% effort 100% of the time. I've sat in meetings where executives thought it was okay if they could achieve 80% of any measurement. So sad. If you don't strive for excellence you'll never, ever come close to achieving it.

Second – don't give your customers an excuse to change. I never understood the practice of charging old customers exorbitant rates while giving new customers discounts and lower prices. Think about this: you're punishing long time customers and rewarding ones with which you have no history. If that sounds dumb – it is. Give your old customers a break once in a while. Maybe even reward them!

Third – treat your customers exactly the same as you would want to be treated. Sounds simple – and it is.

Four – the only true measurement of customer satisfaction is how long they stay with you. If you insist on attempting to measure it then use a meaningful system. Rating from 1 – 10 means nothing on any portion of a survey. I ask: what's the difference between 7 & 8 or 2 & 3? Nothing! Using these types of measurements just allows you to hide true customer feelings. Let's face it – there are only truly three metrics: Bad – Neutral – Good. When you run surveys using only these three possible responses, you'll be shocked – or thrilled - at the results. Executives and managers hate this limitation because they can't hide behind the results. That alone should tell you it's the right way of measuring your customers.

And by the way – most customers will never respond to a survey anyway unless they are upset and dissatisfied and want to let you know it.

All workers have a default level of production

What I mean here is that all employees will work at a certain level they've become accustomed to and probably won't change.

Some will put in a solid 40 hours of productive work and even exceed expectations once in a while.

Some will do the absolute minimum they think they can get away with.

Most will work at a mediocre average level of production of 60-80%.

You will probably not change these people no matter how you incentivize them. Certain people are comfortable at a certain level of effort. Just face it, live with it, and save your money for things you can change.

But you can (and must) try to keep your employees happy and at least as productive as possible.

One major morale builder is letting your workers pick their shift whenever possible. Most companies I worked at were 24 hour operations so we always had three shifts and this idea was a major success – and I admit – it was their suggestion.

Sound crazy? I can tell you people are not designed to constantly have to change their work hours. Rotating shifts is a bad idea and the employees will rarely adapt. Each time someone works different hours they walk around in a daze for weeks. The safety concerns from accidents alone are not worth the risk.

On the other hand, if you ask, you'll find certain people love to work certain shifts. At my employee's suggestion I changed the shifts to 7am-3pm, 3pm-11pm, and 11pm to 7am. This way all of them avoided rush hour traffic. The second shift were a bunch of party people so they went clubbing when they got off work. The third shift were either parents who got home early enough to get their kids off to school and then slept for a few hours or people with second jobs. The day shift was mostly new hires I needed to keep an eye on or were in training.

Pretty soon other executives in my company took notice about how happy and loyal the employees in my department were and how absenteeism plummeted.

While we're on the subject of employees I need to add an important point:

The biggest troublemaker is often the best employee

'Troublemaker' is perhaps the wrong term here, maybe 'problematic' or 'high maintenance' or 'opinionated' would be better choices but you'll probably recognize this person easily enough. This person usually has a bad reputation among other employees or managers. You'll hear comments like 'they don't listen' and 'not team players' and 'they ask too many questions'. Well those are my kind of people.

I'm reminded of certain kids that don't sit still and get into everything – they are usually the most creative, imaginative, and intelligent. Dumb kids sit around like lumps, smart kids are curious and hard to handle.

I've found it's the same in the business world. Hard to handle employees are usually (not always but more often than not) the best employees if you want to get things done. They don't take 'no' for an answer and they take nothing for granted. If you have patience and can harness these types they can make you very successful.

And finally:

Give credit where credit is due.

If (and when) an employee does something outstanding or comes up with a great idea or suggestion – make sure your boss and other executives know it. You will end up looking good because it will be recognized you put together a good team and your employees will respect you and be loyal.

Sales is one of the most important departments

Sure, production, service, operations, and accounting are critical functions – but they can't exist without sales. I can't believe that when businesses start to feel a pinch, sales is the first to be cut. Sales pays for itself - or it certainly should; if it doesn't something is structured wrong.

Sales is the lifeblood of the company. Sales people are the cheerleaders. If you can get that enthusiasm of sales to rub off on the rest of the company you will be amazed. One of the most enlightened companies I worked for made it a point to mingle sales with the other departments as much as possible. Sales would recognize employees in other departments with awards and have them join in dinner meetings. All other department managers attended all sales meetings – which were usually lavish dinner celebrations or golf outings or something fun. In that company sales people were truly cheerleaders and it rubbed off on every employee at every level. And it was spectacularly successful. Sales got almost as many leads from employees as they did from advertising. And you know what? Pretty soon every employee became a proxy sales person.

Every report you see will be wrong in some regard

As I rose through the ranks I became privy to more and more company reports. I can't remember a single one that was 100% accurate in every regard. It was actually frightening – that executives were running a business on faulty information. Every time the data was either meaningless or just plain wrong.

Inventory is usually a joke or a wild ass guess. I can't tell you how many times I've seen worthless inventory carried on the books. At one place a line item was supposed to be worth $112,000. When I checked I found the items were custom made stainless steel housings for TUBE televisions. Items that were from 1996 and will never be used. I managed to get $3,300 from a scrap metal yard for them.

Owners and others love to hoard stuff – and it's all in inventory.

Even if it's legit it's probably wrong – wrongly identified or over bought. You can be almost certain 25% of your inventory is worthless or not needed. Walk through your warehouse sometime and look at the shelves – if there's dust on certain ones you can be sure you don't need it. Even worse are the outside yards were junk always accumulates. If there are weeds growing around and through it then you have a problem – excess junk.

Receivables – if there is any line entry of an account over 90 days past due you have a major problem and can pretty much assume you're going to have to write it off. If someone hasn't paid you in 90 days then you can be assured they got billed wrong or they can't pay you and never will.

This also brings me to another point:

Most company's invoices are wrong

Invoices and bills are cryptic and never provide enough information. I mean you – your invoices are incorrect or lack enough information for the customer to pay them. Luckily most companies are just as lazy so their clerks just blindly pay your invoice. If you get a savvy accounting clerk that knows what they're doing – watch out. They'll use the errors to avoid paying you as long as possible.

Conversely:

Payables - Most companies are improperly billed

Just like your invoices are wrong, so are the people billing you. Remember the story of our telephone bill back in the introduction? Well bank on the fact that most of the bills you receive are in error. In medium and large corporations someone could make a real name for themselves finding all the billing errors.

When I went through the Payables report at one company line by line – over 12 pages – I found all kinds of interesting payments. There were payments to a former owner's sister (for what nobody knew but we had been faithfully paying them for over a year since we acquired the business).

There were payments to a law firm. Turns out that was a settlement of a sexual harassment suit and again we had been paying them even though we did not purchase the former owner's liabilities.

There were dozens of sweetheart deals buried in there too, buying items at exorbitant prices.

Question every line item!

Work in progress – of all the reports in a typical company this one I've found to be the most error prone every time. The labor hours are incorrect, the materials used are incorrect, and the degree of completion is a fantasy. Managers love to fudge this report to make themselves look good.

I once worked for a major Fortune 500 corporation where managers were given incentives based on job completion and profitability. Sounds reasonable, right? Yeah until one day we found out that managers were sending technicians out to jobs to install one part and then calling the job complete even though there was no working system. All these idiots thought somehow after the end of the month they would send someone back to finish the job on a service call, but of course they could never catch up and soon couldn't even keep track of all the unfinished jobs.

In this case the report was pristine, but as I examined it closely I grew suspicious of how the labor hours were too low on many jobs. It was virtually impossible to skew the labor numbers because they were pulled from the payroll system. So I didn't comment at the time, figuring I'd dig deeper into the actual paperwork on some of the jobs.

I never got the chance. A fire inspector showed up at one of our clients and performed a test of the fire alarm. When nothing worked he stood by as a service tech was dispatched and embarrassingly discovered no wires had been installed connecting the fire alarm components. In the rush to close out the job before the end of the month our installer had just screwed equipment to the wall and left. As a consequence this branch was barred from doing any fire alarm jobs in the city of San Jose for years.

This goes to show you if a report looks too good it's probably a complete fabrication.

While we're on this subject there is another aspect that executives love to boast about: **Backlog**. Somehow these people think the longer the backlog of jobs to be done the better. I've sat in many a meeting where every executive and manager in the room was blissfully happy about an eight week backlog. In other words that meant if you sold a job today it wouldn't even get started for eight weeks.

The thinking behind this is supposedly feeling comfortable knowing you have lots of work ahead. Not so good for your customers though – or for your bottom line where you could be billing for completed jobs.

On the flip side are the contractors that start a dozen jobs at once but only show up for an hour or two on each one every week. Instead of hiring enough employees to actually work on all the jobs at once, they just make the customer wait – and wait, and wait.

Most companies are woefully inefficient and wasteful

OMG! I've seen more waste and inefficiency in business than ever in government. At least most government entities have some form of oversight – lax as it may be. In business there are none (except maybe large shareholders).

Waste in business starts at the top. Does the chief executive really need a $30,000 desk and $100,000 in office decor?

Early in my career I figured out if the CEO's office was tastefully but modestly furnished it was going to be a good place to work. Here was a person who cared about the bottom line and didn't waste money. Instead of a $30K desk he bought another vehicle or piece of machinery that was going to make the company money.

If you're the sole proprietor then I guess it's your prerogative to spend outlandish sums on office furniture. If you're an executive of a corporation then it's not your money!

'Oh, but the company is successful and we make a profit', you say. Well, what's wrong with making more profit thereby being even more successful?

And it doesn't end at the CEO's desk. Pretty soon all the executives have expensive furniture. All the office staff have $200 worth of paper holders, staple removers, trays, and every trinket and knick-knack in the office supply catalog – and that's times 25-50 desks or cubicles and suddenly we're talking about real money. I've seen office setups that cost upwards of a half million dollars! That's money that could have gone right to the bottom line or been invested in money making equipment or marketing.

Oh, there is plenty of waste to go around in any business. Retail even has a name for it: shrinkage.

Shrinkage is the line item for waste.

Goods get damaged and thrown away.

Employees steal.

Customers shoplift.

Vendors short you on deliveries because no one checks.

Wrong items are ordered by mistake and never returned so they sit in inventory.

Employees waste hundreds or even thousands of hours.

Every dollar of waste is a dollar of less profit.

The CEO or president needs to lead

I've had the pleasure of working for a few good bosses (far too few), a couple of really bad ones, and a whole lot of mediocre ones. The mediocre leader is in many ways the worst of all.

The 'lead' part of that statement is the most important and the most lacking. CEOs and presidents seem to think their entire job consists of sitting back at their desk and readings reports – oh, and lunch and golf.

Since reports are untrustworthy as we've seen, that's not going to do much to improve the bottom line- unless they are willing to dig into details and just not peruse the totals at the bottom on the page.

The top person needs to be a leader. A leader inspires their workers. A leader needs to have contact with their employees – and I don't mean through some corporate video, I mean in person.

When I became a manager the first thing I did was to drop in on each of my shifts. We were a 24 hour / 365 day operation so visiting all the shifts including weekends wasn't exactly convenient for me, but I felt it had to be done. I remembered all too well the times I worked all alone on graveyard shifts.

The first time I walked in at 10pm and stayed until 2 am, my employees were shocked beyond belief. At first they thought something was wrong. Was the company going out of business? Were they all being fired?

When I assured them that they all had jobs and I just wanted to check in, they were more shocked – and after that – thrilled. They were thrilled their boss would get up in the middle of the night and visit them. They were ecstatic someone cared enough to see how they were doing, how things were going.

I stayed and watched them work. I listened to their problems and concerns and suggestions. I even answered phones and talked to customers. And I didn't stop. I made it a regular monthly thing to drop in at random times on every shift.

News of my visits went through the company like a wildfire. No one could believe it – except my boss, the president. He told me later he wasn't a bit surprised, that was why he promoted me.

The company held regular regional meetings of the management. When it was our turn we took everyone to dinner of course. One of the managers from another region mentioned he'd like to see my operation the following day if I had time.

"How about right now?" I replied.

They all looked at me like I was crazy. "It's past midnight, Ed." One said in disbelief.

"We have nothing to hide. My employees are great. I trust them."

They agreed anxiously. I sensed it was a challenge. I was going to look bad and they could tease me about it forever.

Completely unannounced we all drove over to my office and went in. Just as I expected my people were hard at work. They were very professional at showing the visiting managers around and answering questions. I could clearly sense their pride.

Afterwards none of those managers laughed at me.

A few days later the vice president caught me in the hall. "You got a lot of balls inviting those guys here at one in the morning."

The president, a genuine leader who I always looked up to, overheard the comment and yelled out, "But you sure made us all good, Morawski."

Your employees need to see you

Just like a general leading his troops into battle, ALL your employees need to see you.

Walk the assembly line. Check in on the warehouse. Definitely visit any and all branch offices. If you have employees working at customer's site. Then by all means drop in on them too. At the very least your employees will appreciate it and it will make them feel someone cares and that they are part of the team. You might even learn a few things in the process.

How much do you need to know to run your business?

I don't know where this concept of a CEO as a glorified accountant sitting in an ivory tower, who knows nothing about what his company actually does started, but I'm pretty certain it's not the avenue to true success. There are way too many CEOs who know nothing about what their business actually does. If you manufacture something, shouldn't you at least know how it's done? If you service customers in some way, shouldn't you know the basics of how to do it? If you sell a product, shouldn't you know everything about that product?

People like Bill Gates and Elon Musk and the late Steve Jobs were intimately familiar with every aspect of their business and I believe that's one of the primary reasons they were so successful.

I have to say I very much admire Marcus Lemonis, of the TV show 'The Profit' fame, for his willingness to get his hands dirty and learn how every business he invests in really works.

It might be argued that the only reason business is generally doing well is simply because there are more total consumers now – it certainly isn't because companies are more efficient or better managed.

Apple is not the same company it was when Jobs was running it. He was involved in every level from concept to design to manufacture and sales. Apple is profitable but its future is highly uncertain. Apple is living on its past accomplishments and only makes money because of the number of consumers. There is no innovation coming out of Apple and that will be its death sooner or later. With Jobs and Gates gone Microsoft and Apple are really just cruising on sheer volume. They're living off past success.

When I bring up these points I usually hear something like: "Business is good and we're making money, why should I change?'

Well I would say: 'What's wrong with more business and larger profits?'

7. Is There Such a Thing As Fate?

My favorite subject – and one most people studiously avoid.

What is Fate?

Fate | Definition of Fate by Merriam-Webster

Noun. fate, destiny, lot, portion, doom mean a predetermined state or end. Fate implies an inevitable and usually an adverse outcome. i.e. The fate of the submarine is unknown. Destiny implies something foreordained and often suggests a great or noble course or end.

Meet One's Fate · Cheat Fate · Freak Of Fate · Tempt Fate

https://www.dictionary.com/www.dictionary.com › browse › fate

Fate | Definition of Fate at Dictionary.com

Fate definition, something that unavoidably befalls a person; fortune; lot: i.e. It is always his fate to be left behind.

Is destiny and fate the same thing?

Although often used interchangeably, the words 'fate' and 'destiny' have distinct connotations. Traditional usage defines fate as a power or agency that predetermines and orders the course of events. Fate defines events as ordered or 'inevitable' and unavoidable. ... Fate is often conceived as being divinely inspired.

Religions, especially Catholicism, hates the term 'fate' because it suggests humans have no free will. So they use a different term:

Predestination - Dictionary Definition : Vocabulary.com

In religious terms, predestination is the belief that everything that happens has already been determined by God — He's got a master plan, and there's no deviating from it. ... Predestination is related to the concept of omniscience — meaning God knows everything.

Uh, isn't that exactly the same thing?

Yeah, I could never understand how we were supposed to have free will to choose between good and evil so we could go to heaven, but God already knew if we were going to be good and if we were going to heaven.

Personally I don't believe the negative connotations of Fate. Fate does not mean adverse results. Fate just means consequences or results. Fate just is.

I don't like 'predestination' either. If it's made up by religion it's almost certainly bogus. It implies we have no choice since our choice is already known in advance.

My first real introduction to Fate

When I was in the Vietnam War I was stationed at a small air base in the Mekong Delta. At that time it was very hot with Viet Cong activity. Every night at random times the VC would fire crude rockets into our base. These were not designed so much to kill or maim (although that was a great side effect for them), they were to harass us. It was a form of psychological warfare plain and simple.

After working long hours in the heat all we wanted to do was relax and unwind. But every night at 7 pm or 10 pm or 2 am they would fire their rockets, forcing us to stop whatever we were doing, like playing cards, or chess, or writing letters home, - or even more important: sleeping – and rush outside to a fortified bunker.

I can tell you a few weeks of this really took its toll on us. Not only were we nervous wrecks suffering from lack of sleep but frustrated and angry. And we were all aircraft mechanics so a small mistake while performing maintenance could mean a downed warplane.

At one point one of my friends had enough. He refused to budge when the sirens alerting to incoming rockets sounded.

"If I'm going to die it doesn't matter where I am so I may as well just stay here," he announced to the rest of us.

Somehow I instantly knew he was right. Even at the ripe old age of 19 I had already experienced enough near misses to believe: If it's your time to go, nothing is going to stop it. Fate would determine my future.

Most of the other guys agreed. We never rushed out to the bunkers again. We continued playing Pinochle or chess or writing letters while rockets fell outside. Some guys even sat on the roof watching the rockets explode like it was the Fourth of July.

Were we tempting Fate or were our lives safe because of Fate?

But I'm not interested in all that. I'm so fascinated by Fate because it informs such tenuous connections in human existence.

One tiny change in someone's life can have so many consequences they're for all practical purposes incalculable. Our lives hang by the thinnest threads. One break and not only are our lives changed forever but so are countless others connected to us by Fate.

Have you ever considered: What if?

I'm sure you have. But let me illustrate my outlook with a story. For this exercise we'll invent a character named Tom.

Tom had a normal childhood in suburbia. He is of slightly higher than average intelligence. He had a few friends. When Tom finished college he got a decent job at a small privately held corporation. Tom worked hard and advanced.

Soon he met a nice girl and they got married and bought an average home with nice neighbors with whom they became friends. They had two kids, a boy and a girl. Tom got promoted to manager. Tom and his family lived a comfortable life. Their life was not exceptional in any way but no one complained.

After several years Tom got a lucrative job offer in another state. The only reason he accepted it though was because it was in a much warmer climate and his family was weary of icy cold winters where they presently lived.

Tom moved his family across the country. Before too long his kids grew up and found mates and eventually one had two children of their own, while the other couple adopted a child from another country. (Even this child is a tenuous branch – the kid's unwed mother could just as easily have aborted it. This child's life is already a consequence of a decision.)

Tom and his wife love their grandkids and spoil them as grandparents are wont to do. All three grandkids are cute and handsome and personable and smart. Soon Tom and his wife retire and enjoy the grandchildren more than anything. Life is good.

I won't expand this family further because the possibilities are infinite from this point.

Now we are going to travel back in time twenty years – just before Tom was offered the new job and moved his family.

Consider the possibilities, the alternative outcomes of just this one little family unit:

A new girl comes to work at Tom's company. Pamela is super smart, savvy, and drop dead gorgeous. Tom and Pamela fall madly in love and he divorces his wife. Tom accepts the job and he and his new love move across the country, leaving his kids behind. He and Pamela both get jobs at the new company and get rapid promotions and form all sorts of valuable connections in the local society circles. After a time they start their own business and become multimillionaires.

The consequences are profound and widespread:

Tom's kids never leave town so never met their mates. They grow up despondent over their father leaving and amount to nothing in life.

Their two children are never born. The child from another country is never adopted and lives in poverty, a life ruined and potential unfulfilled.

All the great things they may have accomplished never come to fruition. Who knows what that might have been? Three lives are essentially erased from existence.

So many forks - Tom could have died in a fatal car crash and never met Pamela.

He could not have accepted the job and still lived happily ever after.

But in every scenario except one, three lives and all those who would have followed are still erased from existence.

The possible consequences of any single action are staggering.

Was Tom's action predestined? Was his fate already decided or did he have a conscious hand in it? Did Fate decide or did Tom?

Pamela could have had a flat tire on the day of her job interview and never been hired and never met Tom. Or Pamela could have gotten a job at a thousand other companies. Fate already had a hand in putting Tom and Pamela together.

But the final, critical action was Tom's. Tom had to make the choice: his wife or Pamela.

So wasn't Tom in control of his fate and therefore at least four lives?

He couldn't make an intelligent choice because Tom knew nothing of his future grandchildren. He could ponder the consequences of his actions to a point but not entirely.

And what happened to Pamela if Tom rejected her? She never found true happiness and moved restlessly from job to job, from city to city. Did her unhappiness balance out Tom's and his grandchildren?

The sheer incomprehensible complexity of this points to a Supreme Being manipulating fate to some people. I don't buy that. Why would 'God' or the Supreme Being purposely hurt Tom's family? What future outcome would benefit from this action? It's not impossible that there would be some worthwhile event far in the future caused by Tom leaving his family but it seems unlikely.

And if Pamela's tire did go flat so she missed her interview and never met Tom, I could believe in some outside manipulation. But in this case it all came down to Tom.

The really intriguing thing is that we can never know. Once the decision is made or the action taken, we are locked into that path.

If we had time travel, could we go back and change a critical decision? Some scientists maintain that no past event can ever be changed. In that way are our lives preordained?

According to a current scientific theory, all time exists simultaneously.

The **Block Universe theory** says that our universe may be looked at as a giant four-dimensional block of space-time, containing all the things that ever happen, explains Dr. Kristie Miller, the joint director for the Centre for Time at the University of Sydney.

In the block universe, there is no 'now' or present. All moments that exist are just relative to each other within the three spatial dimensions and one time dimension. Your sense of the present is just reflecting where in the block universe you are at that instance.

The 'past' is just a slice of the universe at an earlier location while the 'future' is at a later location.

Albert Einstein had something to say about this. Special relativity eliminates the concept of absolute simultaneity and a universal present: according to the relativity of simultaneity, observers in different frames of reference can have different measurements of whether a given pair of events happened at the same time or at different times, with there being no physical basis for preferring one frame's judgments over another's. There is no physical basis for a set of events that represents the present because the present is always changing based on decisions and actions of the observers.

There is another way of looking at this:

Time is NOT real: Physicists show EVERYTHING happens at the same time. Physicist Max Tegmark claims the flow of time is an illusion.

TIME is not real – it is a human construct to help us differentiate between now and our perception of the past, this astonishing and baffling theory states.

The concept of time is simply an illusion made up of human memories, everything that has ever been and ever will be is happening RIGHT NOW.

There is nothing in the laws of physics to state that time should move in the forward direction that we know. The laws of physics are symmetric, ultimately meaning that time could have easily moved in a backward direction as it does forward.

How can we reconcile Fate with these theories?

In theoretical physics, the problem of time is a conceptual conflict between general relativity and quantum mechanics in that quantum mechanics regards the flow of time as universal and absolute, whereas general relativity regards the flow of time as malleable and relative.

https://en.wikipedia.org/en.wikipedia.org › wiki › Problem_of_time

Problem of time – Wikipedia

The quantum concept of time was invented by physicist Bryce DeWitt:

"Different times are special cases of different universes"

In other words, time is an entanglement phenomenon, which places all equal clock readings (of correctly prepared clocks - or of any objects usable as clocks) into the same history.

What they're saying is that all time exists simultaneously but in separate universes. And quantum mechanics allows for infinite universes.

So every moment and event that ever was or ever will be coexists right now.

Okay, so what does all this really mean? I'll attempt to use logic – though quantum mechanics defies logic.

People have sayings like: 'The past is the past.' And 'You can't change the past.' And that's probably for a good reason.

I believe the physicists – You can not change the past. The past has already happened (even if every second of the past exists right now), because the observers (us) have already observed it. The past is frozen like blocks of ice. The past can't be altered or changed. We will probably be able to observe and even visit the past (remember all the past exists now) but we can never change it.

There is some compelling evidence that the past has been visited by future people.

This is a photo documented beyond doubt as taken in 1941 with a man wearing modern sunglasses and attire. Some critics maintain these items were available in 1941, but look at the man's face – he clearly has stubble and that just wasn't something people did back then. No man back then would come out in public looking that way, especially not to an event.

The possibility that future people have visited the past and not altered the future is more proof the past cannot be changed.

There is no 'present'. Think about it – the present or 'now' can't exist because before you can measure it, it is already in the past. Even 1 billionth of a billionth of a second is the past. The passing of time is immeasurable so the 'present' really is an illusion.

Note that this is a tenet of quantum mechanics entanglement: the instant you measure or observe something in the quantum world, it is changed. The present is always becoming the past so there can be no present.

That leaves the future.

Some theories propose that all of the future has already occurred because all of time exists at once.

Another theory is that the 'future' consists of all infinite possibilities and outcomes of our decisions and choices.

In this theory Tom and his wife and their grandkids live in one future universe, but Tom and Pamela also live happily together in another universe.

Admittedly this is difficult to get one's head around, but since universes are infinite, this is possible. Each decision or action results in a different timeline universe. Every person's possible decision or action results in a different timeline universe.

So where does that leave us with Fate?

Fate does not affect the past in any way. Your decision or action was completed and the past is frozen.

In the (brief beyond comprehension) 'present' Fate awaits your choice.

Fate obviously only affects the future. Since there are infinite possibilities your choice affects numerous universes. So we do have a free will?

I certainly don't pretend to have the answer. I barely understand quantum mechanics at all. As I said the subject of Fate absolutely fascinates me. I can't help but sense there is a connection between 'fate' and physics, and someday it will become clear.

Until then think very carefully about the consequences of your actions!

In Conclusion

Well we've covered a lot of wildly different topics.

I'm not a professor or expert by any measure. I'm just someone who uses logic and common sense to question these things.

Sure the topics were over simplified. Sure there are a multitude of reasons and answers and alternative theories.

But these were my questions and my theories.

I hope at least a few of them were interesting. I hope even more some opened your eyes (and mind) and made you think.

If nothing else you can try out some of my questions on your friends and get some interesting conversations started.

I'll leave you with my mantra:

Take nothing for granted.

Take nothing at face value.

Don't believe anything until you see absolute proof.

Question everything.

Question everything.

Question everything.

Question everything.

Question everything.

Question everything.

Question everything.

Question everything.

About the Author

Ed Morawski is a veteran of the U.S. Air Force and served eight years in various locations from Virginia to California and Vietnam. He grew up in Cincinnati and presently resides with his family in Southern California where he is an expert in electronic security. He enjoys music, photography, and writing.

See his website at **morawski1**.com

No act of kindness, no matter how small, is ever wasted.

-Aesop, *The Lion and the Mouse*
Greek slave & fable author (620 BC - 560 BC)

Visit us at morawski1.com **and sign up for free stuff!**

Other books by Ed Morawski:

Newhope – a mind bending tale of a small community

FLIT – the true story of teleportation

Afterlife – there are too many people in the world

Bloodsucking Vampires – murdering vampires vs. the LAPD

ALoner – he likes being the last man on earth

Perceiver – a paranormal romance about Remote Viewing

Probe – sexy alien invasion

Goddess of Grass – amazing true historical heroine

www.ingramcontent.com/pod-product-compliance
Lightning Source LLC
Chambersburg PA
CBHW021438210526
45463CB00002B/560